Raquel,
I hope you enjoy
our newest book.

[signature]
6/27/23

PROFILES IN
COMPASSION

*Volunteering for a Meaningful Life:
The Rewards of Helping Others*

Dirk Johnson | Robert Owen Carr

Copyright © 2023 by GSBF Media

All rights reserved.

Distributed by Dust Jacket Media Group
through Ingram Fulfillment Group
in association with GSBF Media.

Printed in the United States of America.

ISBN 978-1-953285-46-1 (hardcover)

For my children,
Amanda, Harlan, Nora and Henry
~DJ

To my mother, Mary Frances Carr
~ROC

TABLE OF CONTENTS

	ACKNOWLEDGMENTS	vii
	PREFACE	ix
1	IT CAN GET LONESOME	1
2	SHOOT HOOPS, NOT GUNS	9
3	THESE ARE OUR PEOPLE	19
4	A STAR IS REBORN	25
5	A BRIDGE TO THE WORLD	35
6	SMALL TALK, BIG CHANGES	41
7	ALL BETS ARE OFF	47
8	NOT ACTING HIS AGE	55
9	UNTIL THE END	65
10	AN ANCESTOR'S WHISPER	73
11	WHENEVER THE CALL COMES	81
12	NO SOLDIER'S FAMILY LEFT BEHIND	87

13	A KID'S BEST FRIEND	95
14	SISTERHOOD	103
15	FROM A BOULDER TO A STONE	107
16	THE KID MADE A MISTAKE	115
17	FEELING COOL AT LAST	121
18	IN THE NAME OF HIS FATHER	127
19	THE GIFT OF A SMILE	133
20	A GUY NAMED SCOTT BAUER	139
21	BLUEPRINTS FOR THE BLIND	147
22	DO I LOOK LIKE THAT?	153
23	SITTING AROUND LIKE A TOAD	159
24	A GUY WITH A CHAIN SAW	165
25	PRIDE AFTER DISGRACE	169
26	LIVING IN FEAR	173
27	ALMOST HOME	179
28	FRIDAY IS TIE DAY	189
	EPILOGUE	197
	INDEX	203

ACKNOWLEDGMENTS

Thanks to Michael McMillan, who designed the cover and pages of this book, and Anne McMillan, who scrupulously proofed and fact-checked its pages, as well as Troy Johnson, who oversaw the marketing and distribution.

Deepest appreciation to those who volunteer their time to help others in need and who took the time to share their inspiring stories for this book. ~DJ

Heartfelt gratitude to all staff members at Give Something Back, whose compassion, loyalty and creativity have nurtured the promise of so many young people who have finally gotten a break. ~ROC

PREFACE

In my circles, I run into plenty of people of retirement age who find themselves searching for meaning in this new chapter of life.

After focusing on work and climbing upward in their careers, many have successfully reached the mountaintop.

But they are left wondering:

Now what?

Some people, especially those who have achieved financial comfort, are content to spend their days relaxing at the waterfront, perhaps with an iced tea or a gin and tonic in hand, enjoying a tranquil and seemingly idyllic reward for their labors.

Good for them.

For my part, rather than head to the beach in my seventies, I amped up my nonprofit organization, which provides college scholarships and career opportunities for disadvantaged kids, and also started an ambitious new business.

While heading a charitable organization isn't for everyone (to say nothing of founding a company), there are countless ways for virtually everyone to use their talents and wisdom for good causes.

In doing good for others, we have the chance to change lives—perhaps even save them—as well as nurture our own.

Throughout the course of American history, volunteerism has been an engine for crucial change. The rise of social reform movements in the 1800s, as civic leader Susan Dreyfus noted in the *Stanford Social Innovation Review*, took on the issues of poverty, addiction, sexism, slavery. These efforts led to the founding of the Underground Railroad, the YMCA, the Salvation Army and the American Red Cross, among other institutions devoted to the simple but noble mission of looking out for one another.

But in recent times, despite being able to virtually reach almost anyone with the click of a keystroke, we are often pulling back from one another. Volunteerism peaked between 2003 and 2005, when nearly 29 percent of Americans reported having volunteered in the past year. But that number has recently dipped to 25.3 percent, according to the Bureau of Labor Statistics.

The decline, which has occurred among all ages, translates to the loss of millions of volunteers—and untapped talent and energy. Particularly worrisome, the drop comes at a time of growing needs for people willing to lend a hand to others. The stakes are especially high as economic inequality has widened and bitter divisions have become a hallmark of contemporary society. We increasingly exist in bubbles with people of our own kind and views, and recoil from those who do not share our ways or sentiments.

As an antidote to such cleavage, volunteerism requires communication and a give-and-take between people from diverse backgrounds who might otherwise harbor starkly different sensibilities. In this way, volunteerism can work as a bridge. It brings together communities in a shared mission and encourages people to see and appreciate one another's humanity.

These good works, as the *Stanford* report points out, form the building blocks of a healthy civil society, in which citizens are "more likely to focus on what unites us than what divides us."

My own pursuit of philanthropy and volunteerism was rooted in a desire to return a long-ago favor. As a senior in high school, I was awarded a $250 scholarship from the Woman's Club in my hometown of Lockport, Illinois.

It came as a wonderful surprise. I had not applied for the scholarship. In fact, I didn't even know it existed. To be candid, I would not logically have been a top choice for the honor, at least based on my academic rank. While I was a good student, I was not at the very top of my class.

I believe the scholarship came my way because a guidance counselor at the school saw potential in me and was familiar with my home life. Like a lot of other people, I had grown up experiencing some troubled times. We lived on a country road in a tiny two-bedroom house crowded with nine people, including my grandmother. My parents were blue-collar people who were unhappy with different areas of their work lives and distrustful of people with advanced schooling—or what seemed to them to be fancy, higher-paying jobs. Neither of my parents wanted me to go to college.

Our home life, meanwhile, was volatile. My father was a hard drinker with a bad temper. He was insulting and knocked me and my younger siblings around. My mother worked nights as a waitress to help make ends meet for many years before she finally summoned the courage to leave him. It wasn't an easy childhood, to be sure, though plenty of others have experienced a lot worse.

When I received the scholarship, my name and picture appeared in the local paper and I was honored with a plaque. The award made me feel special. It inspired me to believe that somebody believed in me enough to invest in me. It changed my life. I vowed to myself that if I ever had extra money, I was going to use it for scholarships for other kids who had endured hardship.

After graduating from the University of Illinois with a bachelor's degree in three years, and earning a master's in my fourth year, I got a fast start on a career. I worked two jobs at once, a position at a local bank and as an instructor at a new community college nearby called Parkland. I was elected to be president of the faculty organization.

Very young and awfully confident, I decided to go into business for myself, certain that I would become a millionaire by age thirty and someday even launch a run for the presidency of the United States.

The reality turned out to be more humbling than my aspirations. In my business enterprise, I struggled for a couple of decades. Times were sometimes so tight that I risked forfeiting my house to foreclosure and losing my car to the repo man.

There were times I thought about giving up, but I hung on and the stars ultimately came into alignment for me. My business soared in value. My company, which specialized in payments processing, went public on the New York Stock Exchange. In my fifties, I had become a wealthy man.

I never forgot what the Woman's Club award meant to me back in 1963. Indeed, a copy of the plaque still hangs in my office after sixty years.

To keep the promise that I had made as a seventeen-year-old—to help kids who could use a break—I established a scholarship program that came to be called Give Something Back. It provided money for tuition and room and board to smart young people who are long on determination but short on means.

From its beginning at Lockport Township High School, my alma mater, Give Something Back would grow into a nationwide program, helping students from New York to California. Over time, it evolved to make special outreach to students who had faced the most severe of hardships, such as foster care, the incarceration of a parent, or the plight of homelessness.

More recently, Give Back has also concentrated on helping students who choose to pursue a trade school or other vocation, often through an associate's degree at a community college. That allows them to hit the ground running with a good paycheck and a marketable skill. These are dignified and honorable careers that are critical to the nation's economy; millions of such positions go unfilled as employers have been unable to find people with the necessary skills.

The payment processing company I created as a start-up in 1997 was acquired for $4.3 billion by a competitor. Rather than retire, I started a new company, Beyond, which is largely owned by Give Back. I donate my $1 annual salary from the business to the nonprofit. It is my hope that profits from the company will benefit disadvantaged young people for many years after I step away.

To date, I have invested a lot of time and more than $85 million in nonprofit causes, mostly to Give Back. These investments have been worth every minute and every cent. It is almost impossible to describe the joy, purpose and meaning that the program has brought to my life.

I continue to serve as its chairman of the board, and few things make me happier than our meetings and annual dinners for our scholars and their proud families, coaches and mentors.

I don't claim to be driven by altruism or selflessness. In fact, I don't believe in the typical use of these two words—but that's another topic. Seeing the difference achieved by Give Back makes me very happy. It is why I encourage people to consider putting their efforts behind a good cause—whether it's tutoring for an adult literacy program, or serving as an advocate for survivors of abuse—coaching a basketball league for youths in an impoverished community, or making visits to elderly people who struggle with loneliness.

To make a difference, you don't have to be wealthy or retired. People often think they are too busy to help. They feel overbooked with work and family obligations. But it's surprising how we might have more time than we think, especially when we give of ourselves.

In what seems like a paradox, research has found that volunteering makes people feel like they actually have *more* time in their schedules. Indeed, Professor Cassie Mogilner of the University of California, Los Angeles has cited studies showing that spending time on others increases one's overall feeling of *time affluence*.

This counterintuitive notion can be explained by the greater sense of *time efficacy* enjoyed by productive people. Those who get a lot done realize how much can be accomplished with their time, and that leaves them feeling less stressed, especially compared to those who might plop in front of the television and then wonder where their time has gone. In other words, the more productive you are with your time, the more time you seem to have. It recalls the old adage: If you want something done, ask a busy person to do it.

Volunteering is good for our skills, health, even longevity. Studies show that those who volunteer have greater executive functional ability, decreased levels of depression, and lower mortality rates. The benefits of volunteering extend to healthier body mass index, reduced levels of inflammation and a decrease in cholesterol levels, as well as improved self-esteem, elevated mood and a deepened sense of empathy.

"A positive lifestyle factor like volunteer work," according to Dr. Rodlescia S. Sneed, of Wayne State University, can "actually reduce disease risk."

It even helps burnish a resume. The *Wall Street Journal* reports that volunteering "makes job applicants look more appealing to a hiring manager."

For all the benefits, the most meaningful reward is making a difference in the lives of others—and bringing more meaning to our own lives. On these pages, volunteers and the people they have touched recount the inspiring stories of what it means to reach out to someone in need—and what it means, too, for those in need to be able to grasp a hand that has been extended to them.

On both sides of the embrace, these are people, whatever their differences, who recognize the fundamental need we have for one another.

~ROC

CHAPTER ONE

IT CAN GET LONESOME

When Pat Cook walked through the front door, Anna Marie's eyes lit up like Las Vegas.

"I'm so grateful to have visitors," the elderly woman told Pat, as she leaned forward in a high-backed chair, a walker standing within reach. "It can get kind of lonesome around here."

More than twenty years had passed since Anna Marie, now in her nineties, had lost her husband, Paul. The two of them never had children and she had been living alone in her small white stucco house on Fortieth Street in Minneapolis for a very long time.

Pat, a tall, slender seventy-five-year-old in jeans, gym shoes and a zip-up blue sweatshirt, told Anna Marie how good it was to see her. He had come to visit, as he does at least once a week, as a volunteer for Little Brothers–Friends of the Elderly, an organization devoted to serving older people who are feeling lonely or isolated.

A former financial planner, Pat had long ago grown weary of a career that focused on "people and their money." He chose to spend his retirement years "giving myself permission to do the kinds of things I find fulfilling—things where I can be heart-to-heart with another person."

Pat had known bouts of loneliness himself. For him, the feeling of isolation came at what would seem a surprising time of life. He was a college student living in a fraternity at the University of Minnesota. But he wasn't having the exuberant, carefree experience that people might associate with campus life. For much of the time, he was alone and drinking.

A pivotal moment came when his fraternity required its members to take on a service project. Pat chose to do his volunteer work at a mental institution.

It hit close to home. He had grown up with a mother who suffered from mental illness and alcoholism. The patients in the institution touched him in a way, he said, that he had never experienced.

"It was the first time," he said, "that I had ever felt such deep empathy."

He came to learn that genuine happiness came from making other people happy. After leaving the personal financial planning field, he went to work in fundraising for Minnesota Public Radio. It was there that a donor told him about Little Brothers of the Elderly.

Little Brothers was founded in France in 1946 by Armand Marquiset to serve the isolated and lonely people who had lost loved ones and even entire families in World War II.

"The greatest poverty," Marquiset believed, "is the poverty of love."

Little Brothers (despite the name, the organization included women as well as men) expanded to the United States in 1959. It grew to seven chapters in the United States, including one in Minneapolis with more than five hundred active volunteers. Some fifty years ago, one of the volunteers for Little Brothers in Minneapolis was August Wilson, who washed dishes for the organization before going on to become a legendary playwright.

Lonely elderly people were often referred to the Little Brothers by an adult child or a health care worker. Some learned about the group on their own and called for companionship, sometimes just looking for someone to talk with over the phone.

As word of the good works of the Little Brothers has spread, their ranks of volunteers and donors has grown, too.

"Half of our budget comes from estates," Pat explained, "and most of it is from people we didn't even know."

The most important mission in Little Brothers (now known as Friends & Co) was simply spending time and socializing. Even in an age when technology makes it possible to connect instantly with someone across town, or on the other side of the world, the burden of loneliness has been worsening, according to U.S. Surgeon General Vivek Murthy, who has described loneliness as a public health "pandemic."

The Census Bureau has found that about 30 percent of people over sixty-five lived in a single-person household. More than 40 percent of seniors reported regularly feeling lonely, according to a study at the University of California, San Francisco. Other research showed that lonely people had a 64 percent increased risk of developing dementia. Coronary bypass patients who reported feeling lonely died within thirty days of surgery at a far higher rate than those with a sense of community.

It was not just an American phenomenon. In the United Kingdom, a "minister of loneliness" was appointed in 2018 to address the problem.

Health and well-being experts have cited serious implications to being chronically lonely that go beyond boredom and feelings of disconnection. Research at Brigham Young University has suggested that loneliness posed health risks equivalent to smoking fifteen cigarettes a day. Loneliness was deemed an even greater health risk than obesity.

Across all age groups, loneliness grew worse during the COVID-19 lockdown. But isolation among the elderly was worsening even before the spread of the virus. In today's mobile society, children frequently move away to follow careers. Spouses die. Friends relocate to another region after retirement. Driver's licenses are surrendered or revoked when getting behind the wheel becomes too dangerous.

To combat loneliness and alienation, Friends & Co organized social gatherings, such as group birthday parties each month, as well as festivities around the holidays. It also staffed a loneliness call line. But its central mission was visiting the elderly at their homes, whether that was a house, an apartment, or a nursing home. Each volunteer was assigned to visit a person at least once a week.

For Pat, who visited several people each month, the volunteer work had become one of the most important elements of his life.

On a weekend, he often made six trips to keep company with the lonely. He might take a person for a drive, go to a coffee shop, or make a stop at an ice cream parlor.

For a retired woman who had been a potter, and whose loss of sight and other frailties brought an end to her work, Pat arranged a visit to a studio, where a group of artisans gave her a rousing round of applause for her accomplishments in the craft.

For Anna Marie, who had become Pat's good friend, he brought a tin of strawberry rhubarb tarts, along with vanilla cherry cheesecake. After he arrived at her home, which had a wheelchair ramp, he slipped into the kitchen to find a couple of bowls. He returned with a big helping of dessert for each of them.

"Oh gosh, this is good!" Anna Marie told him. "You know, when I was growing up, we grew rhubarb in the backyard."

Over the years, Pat had come to learn a lot about Anna Marie's life. She had known hardship from an early age. Her father, an immigrant from Sweden, died when she was seven years old. Anna was only twelve when her mother "went away" to a mental hospital. She died three years after being committed.

Raised by older sisters, Anna Marie was sent to a boarding school in the Minnesota countryside run by the Seventh Day Adventists. Because she couldn't afford tuition, she was required to pick strawberries and beans to pay her way.

"I remember the Depression," she said. "We were poor. Dad died and we didn't have any insurance. We survived on money from the county."

As her mind drifted to the old days, she pointed to photographs on the wall: one of her mother who was hugging a tree, and another of Anna Marie with her husband, Paul. She was then in her thirties, a striking brunette. In her nineties, she was still very pretty. She wore a denim skirt and a blue wrap, her white hair swept back.

Anna Marie and Paul had met and fallen in love in the psychiatric ward of a hospital. She was being treated for depression—"I guess I get it from my mother," she said—and Paul was being treated for schizophrenia.

Both of them were extremely smart. Paul was an associate college professor.

"He had a master's degree in chemistry," Anna Marie said proudly.

After her college days, Anna Marie worked in a secretarial pool, one of the few career paths open to women in those days.

A voracious reader, she once went through a book a day. Until not long ago, a volunteer from the library was bringing her six books each week. These days, she was still receiving a steady supply of new books, but now she would mostly gaze at the covers and perhaps glance over a few pages.

Next to her chair lay a book: *Until the End of Time: Our Search for Meaning in an Evolving Universe*, by the physicist Brian Greene.

With Pat, she talked about books—and just about everything else.

"We discuss politics and religion and current events," she said with gratitude. "We tell each other our life stories. Younger people don't really care about your life story."

She asked Pat if he and his wife, Sandy, had any plans for the weekend.

"We're going to the Hungry Hippie Hostel," he told her. "It's on Lake Superior, in farm country, high on a hill."

"What are you doing up there?" she asked.

"We're just going to enjoy the North Country," he answered.

Anna Marie smiled in reverie.

"My husband and I went up north quite often," she said. "His parents lived in Duluth. We stayed in a town… I can't remember the name. But it was so very beautiful."

Anna Marie wanted to know what Pat had been doing earlier in the week.

"I have a friend who has Parkinson's," he explained, referring to another elder he visits for the Little Brothers.

"What do you do with him?" Anna Marie asked.

"I read to him."

"Oh!" she brightened with curiosity. "What are you reading?"

The Mouse That Roared, Pat told her.

The phone rang and Anna Marie picked up. It was a solicitor.

"I've got company, so I can't talk," she told the caller.

And she hung up.

"Something about a vacation deal," she said, shaking her head.

Pat and Anna Marie sat and nibbled and chatted, as comfortable as two old friends could be.

As she had done so many times before, Anna Marie shared with Pat her fear of being moved to a nursing home.

Pat knew that she had good reason to worry. Health care workers have said they would like to see her move to a facility for the elderly. More than once, she had fallen at home and been hospitalized with injuries.

"They tell me I can't go upstairs, so my bed is on the first floor," she said. "It's not the most comfortable bed, so I usually sleep in this chair or the rocking chair. I know I get forgetful. But I do remember to take my pills."

She paused.

"I sound like I complain too much," she said. "I'm just happy that I'm in my own house and not in a nursing home."

Pat said he had a request.

"The last time I was here, you sang me the Swedish national anthem," he reminded her. "Would you do it again?"

A little embarrassed but a bit flattered, too, Anna Marie began to softly lift her voice:

> "Din sol, Din himmel, Dina ängder gröna
> *(Your sun, Your sky, Your meadows green)*
> "Du tronar på minnen från fornstora da'r"
> *(You believe in memories from ancient times)*

Pat smiled and clapped in gratitude. Anna Marie beamed.

It was soon time for the visit to come to an end.

Pat and Anna Marie each said they looked forward to seeing one another the next week.

He held out his hand to say goodbye. She grasped it with both of her hands and held tight.

"She's in a good place," Pat said, as he stepped out of the house and into the sunshine.

And so was he.

CHAPTER TWO

SHOOT HOOPS, NOT GUNS

Almost game time, John Fuqua left his cinder block office and stepped into the gym, a referee's whistle hanging around his neck, and called for the attention of the players.

"Y'all got a book?" he shouted.

John's basketball league incorporated a book club into its roundball activities. He called it "Books Before Ball," and required the players to read at least one book every two weeks.

The kids, boys and girls ages eight to eighteen, gathered every Monday in the gym for book reports and discussions about what they were reading.

The league also held classes on practical skills, like opening a bank account and balancing a budget. Some of these classes were taught by John's wife, Tasheka.

In this South Jersey city of Bridgeton, riven by street gangs and gunfire, John Fuqua used basketball as a way to reach kids living with hardship and instability—financial woes, dangerous streets, parental incarceration and enduring racism.

"We've got rival gang members here playing on the same team—people who have shot at each other playing on the same team," he said. "In our basketball league, I've never created a first-round NBA draft pick, but I do believe I've prevented some first-degree murders."

John grew up in the dangerous Amity Heights public housing project in Bridgeton. He knew the hurdles and heartbreak that many of these kids had endured, including losing family members to drugs or bullets.

A talented athlete, he had made his way to William Paterson University as a football star, getting an education and escaping the impoverished streets.

And then he came back.

"People needed help," he said. "Somebody's got to do it."

He earned his income working for an insurance company, but he made his living as a volunteer, trying to steer kids and families along the right paths.

His organization, Life Worth Living, created the basketball league as a safe space for kids vulnerable as prey and potential gang recruits by local outlaws on the prowl for "shorties."

In John's game plan, the hard court was an alternative to the shadowy street culture.

"To pick up a basketball, you've got to put down a gun," he said. "In basketball, somebody wins and somebody loses. That's life. But at the end of the game, they're alive."

Bridgeton, fifty miles south of Philadelphia, has long been described as one of the poorest places in New Jersey—with ramshackle neighborhoods, vacant lots strewn with broken glass, empty houses and shuttered stores. It was also one of the most violent cities.

"Outside these walls," said John, "it's chaos."

The basketball league served "as a tool and a template," as he put it. It required hard work, discipline, and the willingness to cooperate with others, even when disagreements festered.

An important part of John's role was conflict resolution, pulling apart two fighting kids and sitting them down in his office, insisting that they find a way to get along.

"A lot of these kids are on the fence," said John. "They can go either way."

Predominantly Black and brown, sometimes angry or alienated, they were young people who fit the cliché of being "at risk" for heading toward trouble. Not everyone took a benign view of the young people from these tough neighborhoods.

John put it bluntly: "There are people who would like to see these kids in prison."

A man with powerful forearms, a baritone voice and an affable manner, John had long ago earned deep respect in a community that tended to be leery of anyone selling anything.

"They know me, they know I changed the narrative of my life," he said, "so they trust me with their kids."

When John was growing up, his father lived five minutes away. He might as well have lived on Mars. He never came around.

His mother, meanwhile, struggled with drug addiction and destructive relationships.

"I watched her being abused and I couldn't defend her," said John.

Frustrated, he took his rage to school.

"I was a menace."

In the sixth grade, he was placed in classes designed to address anger management. He was sent to live with his grandmother until his mother got clean. Through it all, he stayed away from drugs.

"I hated drugs," he said. "They had destroyed my mom, my dad, my aunts and uncles."

By the eighth grade, he had found his way and blossomed. He thrived in sports and studies. He was popular among classmates, elected president of the International Club and vice president of his class.

In high school, he excelled in football, basketball, track and field. On the gridiron, wearing jersey number 35 for the Bridgeton Bulldogs, he was an outstanding running back and linebacker. He was named to the All-New Jersey second team, an extraordinary honor in a state with so many great football players.

Best of all, his mother found her way to sobriety.

"My life turned from being embarrassed when she'd come to my games," he said, "to being proud that she was in the bleachers as my number one cheerleader."

For a family that had overcome so much, the worst tragedy struck on Christmas Eve in 2005.

After receiving a call that a nephew had been shot, John ran to the scene, standing helpless to save the dying young man.

John's mother ran to the scene, too.

Overwhelmed physically and emotionally, she collapsed in the snow and lost consciousness.

John frantically performed CPR on his mom, but it was unsuccessful. She was dead at age fifty-four.

"I'll never forget her trying to take her last breath," John said.

He pledged to devote his life to saving the lives of others, working twenty to thirty hours a week organizing and running the basketball league, among other good causes, and lending a hand to as many families as he could.

John worked hard to counter the common notion in the community that every kid, especially the boys, was going to grow up and play professional sports—starring on television and earning so much money that they wouldn't need any other marketable skills.

"If you're one of these kids, especially in the Black community, you've walked through the first sixteen years of your life being told a lie," said John, who is Black. "You've been told that you can be a celebrity and a star, so you think you don't need to focus on books."

When he talked to the adolescent boys, 70 to 80 percent of them would tell him they planned on playing professional sports. He tried gently to bring them around to reality.

"I've got a five-foot-one, 150-pound kid telling me he's going to play linebacker," a football position that requires players built more like a truck than a bicycle.

John rolled his eyes.

For people of any size, of course, the chance of reaching professional sports stardom was vanishingly small.

In virtually every case, the wannabe star athletes would learn the hard truth sooner or later, and the reality could be demoralizing.

"So, what do you do when you're sixteen and you're faced with that bitter disappointment?" he said. "You probably get angry. You might lash out. You act in ways that aren't good for you."

The sky-high expectations sometimes extended to careers beyond sports, especially if they were seen as a ticket to prestige and celebrity.

"You've got young kids being told they can be an astronaut," he said, "and they're not even good at math."

The basketball league served some five hundred young people a year. John was as much a guidance counselor and a career advisor as he was a basketball commissioner and referee.

"You want to get paid for what you do from the neck up," he has advised his young players, urging them to resist being starstruck by glamour. "Be an engineer, be a mechanic, find a spot in the military, be a skilled trades worker. These are honorable careers."

He also worked to counter much of the talk on the streets, especially among the boys, that manhood was attained by driving flashy cars and juggling as many girlfriends as possible.

"Real manhood," he told them, "is being loyal to your girlfriend, to your wife—it's taking care of your family."

Zebron Bartley, an eleven-year-old basketball player, was one of the young players who had his priorities straight. Now in the fifth grade, he had made the honor roll every semester since he was a kindergartner. He was passionate about basketball, and he wasn't immune to dreams. But if the NBA didn't come calling, he had other plans ready. He was thinking about working in the science field someday.

Even at his tender age, he had already recognized the beckoning perils of the street culture.

"I see people throwing gang signals," he said. "A lot of people out there are getting killed. That's why they should be in here, playing basketball."

Sitting nearby was his proud father, Courtney, a thirty-three-year-old union concrete worker.

"I see to it that he stays busy," his dad said. "In this city, there's trouble around every corner."

With the seconds ticking down and a defender shadowing him, a skinny guard wearing a jersey with the number 3 took a few dribbles, gave a head feint, then launched a shot toward the hoop.

Swish.

The shooter was thrilled, and seemingly a little surprised. He raised his hands to his head and jumped in celebration.

Throughout the afternoon, there would be some more swishes and deft passes, but far more often there were shots that caromed off the rim or the backboard, or sailed wide of everything altogether, the dreaded and embarrassing air ball.

During the games, players exchanged congratulatory high fives. Coaches shouted encouraging words from the bench. Spectators stood along the sidelines—parents and grandparents, aunts, uncles and friends—some of them recording the action with their cell phones.

As the horn sounded the end of play, Fuqua shouted to players on both the winning and losing teams, "Good game!"

In this league, the kids played hard and they played to win. But coaches knew that John enforced a strict rule about the importance of sharing court time among all of the team members. Everybody got to play, no matter the level of his or her talent.

A mural on the wall of the gym depicted the basketball star, Magic Johnson, alongside a painting of the writer Lorraine Hansberry—an unmistakable statement about the importance of books for the ballers.

One young player showed up seriously late for his game. When he was told he could not take the court right away but would need to sit on the bench for a while, he glowered.

At the break, John called the player with the sour attitude into his office.

"You need to be where you're supposed to be—at the time you're supposed to be there," he told him.

John was talking about more than basketball.

Like so many of the others in the gym, the young man was coming from a home life with plenty of troubles.

"He's only thirteen years old and he's probably the best player out here," John said, and then lowered his voice in a tone of dismay and with a look of concern. "His dad is in a gang."

John was not about to give up on the young man, who seemed to be listening to his advice.

"He agreed to sign up for summer school," John said.

To John, that was a far better move than anything the baller could showboat on the basketball court.

Basketball was a way to get families in the door. Once inside, it was impossible to miss the messages of help and hope.

On the sidelines, tables were stacked with pamphlets, posters and sheets of paper, offering guidance and assistance to anyone who asked.

> *Has someone you know been in a recent fight?*
>
> *Has your child had a recent argument or disagreement that has you concerned?*
>
> *Has your child begun to pull away from authority?*
>
> *Do you see changes in the behavior of a youth that has you concerned?*

*If you answered YES to any of these questions,
Call Life Worth Living at (856) 420-LIFE
WE CAN HELP!!!*

After the basketball tournament, disaster struck the Bridgeton area.

Gunfire erupted at a Saturday night party. Three people were shot to death, including a nineteen-year-old girl. Nearly a dozen others were wounded, including one of John's cousins, who was shot in the stomach and was rushed to a hospital for treatment.

It had been a Nineties theme party, with people wearing costumes, having a fun and peaceful time.

"And then you get a handful of idiots with guns," John said.

There were kids as young as fifteen at the party. When the shooting started, a nephew of John's ran for his life into the woods, stepping over a body. Others dove under cars.

As police officers performed chest compressions on a bloodied victim, a woman nearby wailed into the darkness:

"Oh my God, she's gone!"

For John Fuqua and Life Worth Living, the mission to save kids and families would continue.

"We can't go home and bury our head in the pillow and wish things away," he said. "We've got work to do."

CHAPTER THREE

THESE ARE OUR PEOPLE

Sherry Brick, a delightful and witty eighty-year-old woman with a beautiful shock of white hair, was busy handing out treats and drinks at a bash for families who rarely got a chance to go out, at least without being stared at.

"It takes so little to make these kids smile," said Sherry, who volunteered twice a week for a group called Bounce Children's Foundation, which organized the party and other recreational events for severely disabled kids, their siblings and parents—people who were often deprived of a social life.

The tiny, kindly Jewish grandmother reached around the shoulder of a boy in a wheelchair, offered a cookie, and then whispered in his ear something that made the kid laugh in the unselfconscious way that every kid ought to be able to laugh.

Sherry grew up on the South Side of Chicago, the daughter of a man who ran a bowling alley. That's where she met the love of her life.

"My husband would tell everybody he met me in the alley and took me out of the gutter," she said with a smile.

She wore a blouse with prints of French bulldogs, just like her own beloved pup, Mshugi (short for *meshugana*, a Yiddish word that loosely translated to crazy). MSHUGI were the letters on her late husband's license plate. Her kids gave her the dog after he died. And so that explained the pup's name.

"Do you want to see a picture of my puppy?" she said, pulling out her phone. "I've got a thousand of them."

Sherry lost her husband a decade ago to Parkinson's. It was not the only hardship she had endured. She lost one son in his thirties to an aneurysm and another at age fifty-three to liver cancer. Her eighteen-year-old grandson, whom she described as "a great joy," was living with autism, unable to speak for much of his childhood.

As someone who had experienced difficult times, Sherry had a real passion for the Bounce families who endured isolation because of the difficulty in going to a restaurant or a movie theater with a child who screamed uncontrollably or pounded on a table.

At the Bounce events, though, these families knew they were not alone. They didn't need to worry about creating a scene.

"If a child screams out here, so what!" said Sherry.

These were families who were grateful for so little, as Sherry observed, and they were surrounded by cheerful volunteers eager to do whatever they could to let them have a little fun—and a respite.

It was an atmosphere that made Sherry's heart sing.

"You watch the news and it's so depressing, and then you come to an event like this, and you know there are good people in the world," she said. "There's nothing better."

"Having lunch with the ladies is fine," she said. "But you need to do something with your life. I need to put smiles on kids' faces. And volunteers are the kinds of people I want to be around—the kinds of people I want to be friends with."

As Sherry worked the food stand, the brothers and sisters of disabled kids—and some of the disabled kids themselves—played laser tag, jumped in the bouncy house, and just ran around or whirled about in wheelchairs, laughing with a sense of innocent abandon.

Kevin and Aidan Taylor, who were eleven and six, respectively, were among the kids running freely at the event inside the site of the Bounce event, a fitness club in Chicago. Their sister, Kyleigh, who was nine and severely disabled, sat in a special chair at a table between her mom, Bridgette, and her dad, Jim.

Kyleigh was born with a condition so rare and complicated there is no name for it, other than chromosomal abnormalities. She cannot walk, talk, or feed herself. Her parents spoon-feed her, or she takes nutrients through a feeding tube that goes into her stomach. She has chronic lung and kidney problems. She has undergone cranial facial surgery. In her young life, she has spent four or five days each year in the hospital.

She attended a special education program at her public school in suburban Arlington Heights. Her parents said it was difficult to measure her cognitive abilities, given her other difficulties, but doctors had estimated it to be about half of what would be expected for the normal range for her age.

"But she's very expressive," said Bridgette, who was a social worker, wearing a t-shirt emblazoned with the words "Strong Mama."

"She can get her point across."

With her brown hair pulled back in a ponytail, Kyleigh wore a t-shirt with the likeness of Queen Elsa from the Disney movie, *Frozen*.

"Is Queen Elsa your favorite?" her mom asked.

Little Kyleigh nodded vigorously.

Bridgette said no tests during her pregnancy had indicated that Kyleigh would have any problems. But when Kyleigh was born, her mother looked at her jaw and was alarmed.

"I knew right away," said her mother, "that something was not right."

Like many others at the Bounce event, the Taylors were generally reluctant to go to public events, afraid they might make other people uncomfortable if Kyleigh acted up, made loud noises, or needed to be fed through a tube.

For them, Bounce was an oasis.

Their first Bounce event was a gathering at a pumpkin patch. When Kyleigh was being fed by her dad, she vomited forcefully into the air, as she does frequently. It was the kind of thing that would cause alarm, or at least unease, if it were to happen in most public settings.

But the man behind them, who also had a child with a severe disability, simply smiled and spoke loudly in an encouraging voice: "Now, that was a good one!"

His words immediately made Jim relax and feel that he was at home with families who could relate.

"I thought, 'These are our people,'" said Jim, who is an occupational therapist in the public schools. "They get it. You don't have to explain things. We knew right then that we were in the right place."

Through the Bounce gatherings, families forge friendships that last beyond the organized get-togethers. They have become close friends with other couples they met through Bounce events. When one of the families has a child in the hospital, for instance, another family will bring home-cooked meals to the house.

"We actually talk at home about our Bounce family," said Jim. "The families and the volunteers have all become part of our life. And the kids will often ask about them."

The Bounce families and volunteers interact easily around Kyleigh.

"Other people tend to see the disability first," said Jim. "At Bounce, people talk *to* her. They don't look *past* her."

Most parents just hire a babysitter when they want a night out. But for people like the Taylors, it wasn't realistic to hire a sixteen-year-old sitter to care for a chronically ill child. Some of the parents who came to Bounce events said they had not been on a "date" in four or five years.

Siblings of those with severe disabilities faced difficult challenges of their own. For unavoidable reasons, they were rarely the center of their parents' attention.

"Anything we do," Jim explained, "we think first of Kyleigh."

With Kyleigh's challenges, young Kevin had grown up as an extremely protective older brother. As his dad put it, "He's more responsible than we'd like him to be."

Kevin has said that when he grows up, he wants to be a 911 dispatcher, an unusual aspiration for a young boy. But he was a kid with experience in navigating dire situations.

"Getting through a crisis," his dad noted, "is something Kevin is used to."

Families with such challenges need to strategize to care for the ailing child and the others. When Kyleigh needs to go to the hospital, Jim takes charge on the medical front while Bridgette stays home with the boys. They prefer not to subject their sons to a hospital so frequently. It was a lot to handle.

But Kevin, nicknamed Bubba, would protest vigorously if he were left home when Kyleigh went to the hospital, insisting that he needed to go and "make sure she is being taken care of."

His dad would tell Kevin: "That's our job."

When Jim and Bridgette look over the ways their life has changed since the birth of Kyleigh, they reflect on the issue of character.

"Our lives were turned upside down, but so were our sons' lives," said Jim. "That's, unfortunately, our reality. But we're grateful that we have two very respectful and compassionate boys. We're very proud."

Kyleigh and Kevin have an extremely close bond. One of the only words that she has ever uttered is "Bubba."

"When she's in the hospital, she doesn't call out for Mom or Dad," said Jim. "She calls out for Bubba."

CHAPTER FOUR

A STAR IS REBORN

For a cool kid in Texas, big dreams were coming to life.

Alex Mutti, who was coming of age in a fashionable, high-stepping stretch of Dallas, had won the coveted role of Babe in her high school production of *Crimes of the Heart*, the Pulitzer Prize-winning drama.

Still only an eleventh grader, she seemed to have it all: talent, wit, charisma, beauty.

Beyond all that, she would be headed to a college where stars were born, New York University, just a heartbeat and a short subway jaunt from Broadway. She would major in theater. She seemed destined for the bright lights.

But in truth, on stage and off, she really was just acting.

After leaving the dress rehearsal for *Crimes*, the night before the big opening performance, she came home to await the curtain call. It should have been a time of triumph, pride and excitement.

Instead, she spent the night sobbing, binging and purging.

When the clock neared one thirty in the morning, she crept into her mother's bedroom and gently awakened her.

"I have something to tell you," Alex said. "I can't say it. But I think you know what it is."

Her mother did not hesitate.

"You have an eating disorder," her mom said, and reached out to hug her daughter as if she would never let go.

"She had me crawl into bed with her," Alex recounted, her voice cracking with emotion. "She told me she loved me. She told me she would be there with me to fight this."

Alex's bouts with anorexia and bulimia had started at age twelve. Her struggle did not end with coming out to her mother. It did not end with the treatment that followed. She battled the disorder for nearly a decade.

At twenty-six, free of any symptoms of the illness for nearly five years, she was giving back. From her small apartment in New York City, she volunteered more than twenty hours a week for the National Eating Disorders Association. She fielded calls and texts from people who were in crisis, or from those who were helplessly watching a loved one struggle.

Some callers were desperate. Many sounded hopeless. Others were angry.

"There's a lot of shame and embarrassment," Alex said. "They think they're the only ones who are dealing with this."

At the other end of the line, there might be the voice of a confused twelve-year-old, or a scared parent, or an eighty-five-year-old who had struggled with eating disorders for more than sixty years.

"Yesterday, I got a call from a fourteen-year-old who was having fainting spells and heart palpitations," said Alex, who urgently advised the girl to seek medical help as soon as possible.

Eating disorders could be deadly, disabling and costly. They posed the second highest mortality rate among all mental health problems, after opioid addiction.

For caregivers, often a parent, the pressure and dread could be overwhelming. Researchers have found that the level of stress and worry for a caregiver looking after a loved one with eating disorders ranked as even more burdensome than caring for someone with depression or schizophrenia.

People with the eating disorders have likely gone through hell before they finally call for help.

"Some will call in tears and acknowledge they have an eating disorder and say: 'What do I do? I want to get help now!'" said Alex.

These are the easiest of the calls.

For those who spoke directly about needing help, Alex was able to immediately gather contacts for therapists, dietitians, physicians and psychiatrists in their regions with expertise in eating disorders. If the caller lived in a deeply rural region, there were teletherapy options.

Often, it was a matter of finding supportive environments that were most comfortable for the caller.

"There is the thirty-year-old trans woman who wants to be in a nonjudgmental group," she said. "And the sixty-two-year-old man who doesn't want to be in a group of teenage girls."

In many cases, callers were not ready for help, often in deep denial that a problem even existed.

These were much harder cases.

"I don't have an eating disorder," insisted one teenager, who complained that her family members were needlessly worried about her. "I don't know what they're talking about."

"Why do you think they might be worried?" Alex nudged.

"So I go three days without eating," the caller replied, with a sigh of exasperation, "but it's just fasting."

Others conceded that family members or friends had found evidence of purging in the toilet, or realized that the household supply of laxatives had gone missing.

As a volunteer, and not a professional therapist, Alex was not allowed to share her personal history with the callers. But she could offer support, encouragement, and a road map to help.

In the public mind, the image of a person struggling with anorexia or bulimia tended to be an affluent white teenage girl. And there were plenty that fit that description. But it could be misleading, since this was also the demographic that was most visible, largely because they came from families with resources and connections needed for treatment. As Alex knew from her volunteer work, eating disorders affected boys and men, too, and touched every age, race, ethnicity and income level.

"People think it's about food, but it's not," she said. "These are mental health issues. It revolves around control. People feel like they are in an uncontrollable, inescapable struggle."

While almost everyone has experienced issues with body image, said Alex, people with eating disorders often had an obsession to be skinnier and skinnier, even when they were already far below a healthy weight.

"People will sit and shake their legs to try to burn calories," she said. "It's *all* they think about *all* the time."

Images on television, the movies, magazines and social media could be triggers that worsened the condition. Some people did not even concede that their eating disorder was an unhealthy behavior. Remarkably, some even called the helpline to ask for tips about how to quickly lose a lot of weight.

"In American culture, there is an ideal of what you should look like—a TV image," she said. "But that's not even real. Those people on the screen don't *really* look like that. The images have been airbrushed and edited."

Just the other day, Alex had fielded a call from a twelve-year-old who was deeply worried about an eating disorder involving her nineteen-year-old sister.

"We've been trying everything to convince her to get help," the younger sister told Alex. "We're desperate."

The reality, Alex told her, was that people usually could only be helped when they were ready to accept help. She urged family members themselves to focus on staying as healthy and emotionally stable as they could.

"How are *you* taking care of *yourself*?" she would ask. "I try to validate how they're feeling. They're overwhelmed. They're stressed. They're putting everything on hold. They've had their lives turned upside down."

Many of the callers suffering from the illness simply wanted to talk to someone who could relate to their lives, even if they weren't ready to take steps to address the problem.

"Often, they have no hope of getting better," Alex said. "They're not even looking for treatment. They feel stuck with the illness. They reach out because they want someone who is understanding."

But with every call, Alex saw hope for recovery.

"Although they're in denial, they *did* reach out to us," she said. "So there *is* a small part of them, somewhere in there, that is dealing with this. We try to get them to open up about why they are exploring it with us."

Others were looking for a silver bullet—either for themselves or a family member—some magic words that would fix everything. And when the magic was not forthcoming, some callers would lash out.

Thanks for nothing!

Is that all you can do?

Why did I even bother to call?

For the volunteer working the helpline, it was important to remember that these were people experiencing terrible pain and not always seeing their circumstances with a clear view.

If there was a single truth that Alex hoped to convey to all of the callers, it was this:

"You are worthy of help and support."

That was not what people with eating disorders were accustomed to hearing.

"An eating disorder is like a voice in your head," said Alex. "But it's not *your* voice. It has separate wants and concerns."

For years, Alex heard that voice herself.

Growing up as a girl who aspired to go into acting, as well as a fan of television and movies, she came to realize that she had long been "taking in a lot of toxic media."

"I believed I needed to look a certain way. My focus on weight, body image—it took precedence over everything, took happiness out of everything."

She would cancel plans with family and friends so she could spend the night at the gym, devoting hours to burning calories.

She would cut herself. She entertained suicidal ideation.

When family and friends found evidence of purging, they tried to confront her.

As a defensive mechanism, Alex would sometimes lash out.

"I wasn't always kind," she said.

She got into a fight with a friend who pleaded with her to get help.

"You don't eat!" the worried friend told her.

After Alex acknowledged her problem, her mother moved to get her into treatment immediately.

The program involved three or four days a week of intensive work: therapy, nutrition counseling, support groups.

Alex marked an upcoming birthday by going to a Wendy's with others in the support group.

"I chose whatever on the menu had the fewest calories," she said. "Some pitiful salad."

But it was the first time in a week that she ate and did not purge.

Every Wednesday for lunch, the people in the support group, along with a dietitian, would eat lunch together and talk about their feelings while they ate.

She did well for a while, but as her senior year in high school began, the symptoms started creeping back, though less frequently. After graduation, she enrolled at NYU and started her major in theater. And then she lost her champion.

Midway through Alex's freshman year in college, her mother died of a heart attack. She was fifty-nine.

"My mom was my biggest cheerleader, my biggest supporter," she said.

Without her mom, Alex closed up and isolated herself. Her eating disorder worsened.

"I went out with a girlfriend and she said: 'You are so skinny! I want to look like you! What do you eat for lunch?'"

"Nothing," Alex told her in a moment of bracing honesty. "You have to have a mental illness to look like this."

Midway through her junior year, she traveled home to her family in Dallas for Christmas, obviously very underweight.

"My sister told me, 'I can tell you are struggling. I'm here when you want to talk.'"

Alex vigorously denied that anything was wrong. But three months later, she called her sister, sobbing.

"You're right," Alex confided.

Her sister and father helped her find a therapist—the same therapist she sees to this day. She was diagnosed as "body dysmorphic."

"I was not able to see the same things that other people were seeing," she said. "I was seeing the same body, a skinny girl. But I believed I needed to get even skinnier. If I'm bigger, I thought I was worthless, that people wouldn't like me."

Between college graduation and graduate school at NYU, she waited tables and auditioned for acting work.

Her therapist grew very worried about her—and frustrated. He threatened to drop her as a client.

"I can't help you anymore unless recovery is your number one priority," he said.

She knew he was right.

"I realized that acting might not be the healthiest line of work for me," she said.

In an acting class, she recalled a casting director admonishing the women in the class:

"Ladies, you have to have the right body."

Alex did not disagree.

"He wasn't wrong," she said. "That's how the industry works. Appearance rules."

Alex decided to follow another path. She would go to graduate school to study social work.

She hoped to work in eating disorders therapy, especially with adolescents.

"I would like to share the truth that it *does* get better," she said.

Her volunteer work with people with eating disorders, she said, "means everything to me."

It had been a difficult journey, and perhaps one that saved her life.

"To be someone who was at rock bottom and never thought they would be able to crawl out," she said, her voice breaking, "and to now be someone who can tell others they are not alone, that they have nothing to be ashamed of."

It was impossible to know how many lives had been changed, or even saved, by Alex's volunteer work. But she saw herself as the lucky one.

"It has changed my life in so many ways," she said. "I have learned how to be a better listener, a better friend."

CHAPTER FIVE

A BRIDGE TO THE WORLD

The sign outside the little house in a small town in Indiana read: "A U.S. Veteran Lives Here."

John Gardner, eighty-four and frail, sat in a chair with a shawl across his lap and a walker nearby.

During the Cuban Missile Crisis, he was on the beach in Florida during the standoff between the United States and the Soviet Union, as the world teetered on the brink of nuclear war.

"We were ready to go," John remembered. "Any minute."

These days, John was confined to his house. His gout and arthritis were so severe he was unable to get out of bed without the help of his daughter and son. Just a few weeks before, he was carried on a stretcher to an emergency vehicle and taken to a hospital.

It was too dangerous for him to climb the porch stairs, or to be pushed in a wheelchair down the steps.

John's daughter, Kimberly Line, made some phone calls to ask if a social services agency might be able to help a low-income senior afford a wheelchair ramp.

She found the Retired & Senior Volunteer Program (RSVP), a group of relatively handy retired men who traveled around Southern Indiana and installed ramps for those of modest means.

Within two weeks of the call, she heard the sounds of sawing and pounding outside the house, which sat on a narrow lot beside a gravel drive and a cyclone fence.

From his chair, John peered through the picture window, the soft autumn sunrays slanting through the pane, and watched as the volunteers built a ramp that would liberate him from being trapped inside his home.

"This will expand my life," said John, who had lost his wife just a few months earlier. "I'm so appreciative."

His voice cracked and then he broke down in tears.

This was a bridge to the outside world. It calmed worries about a fire or some other emergency that would have been impossible to escape.

His children would be able to keep the promise to their dad that he would be able to stay in his home for all of his days.

"There will be no nursing home," said his son, John David Gardner, who was adopted as an infant and still talks with heartbreaking gratitude about being saved by loving parents. "You'll be here at home."

As the son and daughter grew emotional, Kimberly pointed toward the window at the volunteers and gave thanks.

"You don't always realize it," she said, "but there really are good people out there."

None of the six volunteers from RSVP had been trained as carpenters. One was a mechanical engineer, another was a pharmacist, still another was a commercial airline pilot. One man had worked at a General Electric plant.

The team leader was Gary Purlee, a seventy-seven-year-old retired mechanical engineer, wearing a ball cap, gloves, work boots and a hooded windbreaker.

Gary, a graduate of a two-year trade school who worked his way up to management at a plastics company, was a veteran himself, having served in the U.S. Army at Fort Hood, in Texas, and in the Vietnam War. He had been volunteering to build ramps for fourteen years.

He grew up on a farm in Indiana, the youngest of seven children. He got started with the ramps at the suggestion of an older brother, who had done some volunteering for the crew.

"What are you doing on Tuesday mornings?" his brother had asked him.

"Nothing," Gary replied.

"How about coming to build wheelchair ramps?"

Gary didn't have to think for long. All of his life, he had felt grateful for what he had and wanted to help those who were less fortunate. During his engineering career, he had been too busy to do much of anything besides work. As his father grew older, moreover, Gary was needed to help his dad at the farm, so that took up any spare time.

Once in a while, people would tell Gary they were puzzled that he worked building wheelchair ramps on Tuesdays when he could be relaxing or out playing golf.

"I can play golf on Wednesdays," he has replied. "I garden. On the weekends, I walk in the woods. I have plenty of time to do other things."

On this chilly November morning, he was instructing his crew of fellow volunteers how to follow his mental blueprint for the ramp.

"Put the two-by-six right here," he told one of the men carrying a timber beam.

"You bet," came the reply.

"And the four-by-four sits here," Gary told another volunteer.

"Got it," the man answered.

The men carried beams, plunged into the earth with a posthole digger, ran a power saw to cut the timbers laid across a sawhorse, and used a level to make sure everything was standing true.

And they made plenty of small talk—sports, the weather, their grandchildren.

"That Indiana-Purdue football game," said one fellow. "Not quite sure who to root for and who to root against."

Family was never very far out of mind.

"My grandson is thirteen," one of the volunteers mentioned, "and my granddaughter is twelve going on twenty."

Another volunteer spoke up about the hurricane in Florida and the story of a poor woman who lost her roof and was living under a ceiling of plastic.

"I just put up a new roof myself," said a fellow worker, mixing small talk with a nod to mortality. "That'll be the last one I ever have to worry about."

The RSVP crew had two volunteers who worked into their nineties.

"Even if you can't bend over, you can still help," said Gary.

As one of the volunteers put it: "We're just seniors looking for a purpose."

The men might have been a step slower than they were a generation ago, but on this job, there was no boss, no rush.

There was also no paycheck. The men donated their labor. The people who were getting the ramps were asked to pay what they could for the materials, mostly boards and nails, if they could manage. If they couldn't, that was fine.

In some cases, someone had already tried a hand at building a wheelchair ramp but didn't quite make the grade, so the volunteers would take it down and start over.

"Sometimes a brother-in-law or a friend has tried to build a ramp," said Gary, referring to some of the well-intentioned efforts that fell short. "They tried their best."

The RSVP crew followed the local building codes and the guidelines issued by the Americans with Disabilities Act. The size of the ramps built by the volunteer crew ranged from six feet to seventy feet. The lumber typically ran $20 to $25 per foot.

The RSVP project was funded partly by a federal grant from AmeriCorps, along with private donations and a fundraising event.

By far, most of the funding, however, was the in-kind contributions of the labor donated by the ramp builders.

In some cases, they were donating more than their labor. More than once, when a "customer" could not afford to pay for the lumber, Gary had reached into his own pocket to pay for the materials.

"These aren't people living in half-million-dollar homes," Gary explained. "And I'm not the only one who has paid from my pocket. The other guys have, too."

He said the real compensation was knowing they have made someone's life a little better, and then, of course, there was the gratitude expressed by the recipients and their families.

"They'll call and send cards, telling you they can now get to their doctors' appointments," said Gary. "I got a call from a son, telling me over and over, how much easier it was to push his mother in and out of the house. That makes it all worth it."

The director of RSVP, Ceil Sperzel, herself a volunteer well into retirement age, assigned the jobs, handled the bookwork, and arranged for charge accounts at the hardware store. A team would visit a house to see what materials would be needed.

With his list of needed supplies, Gary or another team leader would go to the store with a trailer hitched to his pickup truck and load the materials. He was authorized by RSVP to sign for the materials.

It was a cheerful crew. In Ceil's view, seniors who volunteered for others were happier and more fulfilled than those who focused on themselves.

"It helps you live longer," she said. "There's a lot of stats on that. But if you want a hardcore reason to do it, it gives a person a reason to wake up in the morning and think, 'It really does matter if I get out of bed right now.' You can lay around until eleven o'clock, but that's not really good for you. And it can start a downward spiral. Put our phone number by your bed and one morning you'll call us. And we'll find something for you to do."

John Gardner, the former Air National Guard vet who had been rescued by the ramp builders, was already imagining brighter days ahead.

"I'll be able to go and sit outside when it's nice," he said. "I won't have to call someone every time I need to go somewhere. I'll be a lot more independent, that's for sure."

When the volunteer crew was finished with the ramp, the men headed out for hamburgers, their usual ritual after finishing a job.

If they felt tired or sore, they did not mention it.

CHAPTER SIX

SMALL TALK, BIG CHANGES

While others might comment on the weather, or maybe last night's ball game, David Ambroz broke the ice by raising a personal topic.

"Did you know that Marilyn Monroe was a foster child," he might mention, seemingly out of the blue, "and Nelson Mandela, too?"

It could catch people off guard. But if it made them think for a moment about the 450,000 children in foster care in the U.S., David considered his mission, if not accomplished, at least recognized.

A volunteer advocate and crusader for homeless children and those who were wards of the state, David founded FosterMore, a nonprofit organization that urged people to "Donate Your Small Talk" to raise awareness about the struggles of these young people who faced the most daunting of odds.

Those who have experienced foster care or homelessness were among the least likely to graduate from high school or go to college. They were far more likely than others to become homeless, to go to jail, or to attempt to take their lives.

FosterMore inspired people to do something that would make a difference, big or small, from becoming a caregiver or mentor, to simply asking the local school district what accommodations they were making for the foster kids in their ranks, and then pressing them to do more.

It would make a big difference, David believed, if people would merely speak up about the promise and the challenges for foster kids.

"What gets talked about is what gets done," said David. "If it's invisible, nothing gets done."

Removed by the state from homes where they endured abuse or neglect, these kids were often shuffled around from foster home to foster home, carrying all of their possessions in a plastic garbage bag, nervous about what the next stop would bring.

At a tender age, David Ambroz learned firsthand about homelessness and foster care. Many years later, he would write about his experiences in a book, *A Place Called Home*.

At age five, David would walk the streets of New York in the bitter cold alongside his six-year-old brother and seven-year-old sister, led by their mentally ill mother. He recalled that his feet would grow so numb on the wintry sidewalks that they felt like stubs. The family took temporary refuge in subway cars, hospital waiting rooms, bus stations, Pennsylvania Station, a Bowery slum. They bathed in public restrooms and stole food to stave off hunger.

Their mother would be stoic, not looking at her children or speaking to them for hours, then grow angry, seemingly for no reason. At any moment, she could fly into a rage.

Is she going to hit me? young David wondered, as his mother glared at him. *I can usually tell—but not tonight.*

After the authorities finally intervened, the siblings found themselves in a courtroom. A lawyer asked David if he knew why he was there. His answer was both tragic and terrifying.

"My mom can't care for us. She's sick. I don't feel safe with her. She beats us. We have no food. We barely go to school. She's going to kill me if you put me back there."

Placed in foster care, David would come to learn that some caregivers were more caring than others.

For a gay kid in foster care, being judged was a common experience. As David grew older, he tried to cloak any behavior or mannerism that would suggest he was anything other than a straight boy.

"But they could tell," he recalled.

He recounted being ridiculed by a foster dad named Buck, who would parrot what David would say and make fun of him with an invented mocking lisp.

As David would later write, Buck and the foster mom, Mae, never sat him down and said, 'You are gay and we're going to fix you,' but they found something wrong with "everything I do: how I speak, dress and act."

Buck and Mae eventually arranged for David to undergo a battery of tests and counseling that seemed very much like conversion therapy. The sessions were especially focused on how David presented himself and whom he liked.

"The unspoken goal," he wrote, "is to make a hetero out of me."

In one foster home, David would finally find acceptance, with Holly, a counselor at the YMCA, and her husband, Steve, a building contractor. They fixed up a room for him in the basement and reminded him, time and again, that *their* home was also *his* home.

"Not only am I allowed to roam freely," David would later recall, with wonder and gratitude for the simplest of things, "I am also allowed to eat whatever I want, whenever I want."

In a remarkable journey, David would go on to college at Vassar and law school at the University of California, Los Angeles. He rose to become an executive at Disney Television and then Amazon. He served as the president of the Planning Commission for the City of Los Angeles.

As an unpaid advocate, he helped shape government policies intended to keep foster kids from getting lost. He forged agreements with businesses, too, that promised to cultivate a foster-friendly atmosphere by providing parental leave during the placement of a child, among other benefits. Warner Bros. Discovery made the pledge, along with the Pritzker Group, Beyond, and the Give Something Back Foundation.

David knew from experience that foster youths tended to move frequently, which often interrupted their studies. If, as an example, a student took eight weeks of algebra, falling short of a full semester, and then transferred to another school, that child would lose credit for the work completed at the old school and fall behind at the new school.

That could result in a delay on the path to graduation. For foster kids, time was money. When they aged out of the system, sometimes as young as eighteen, they often lost financial support. It was important to graduate before the clock ran out.

Giving his time and talent for no pay, David would play a key role on an advisory panel in California that drew up a policy, later implemented by thousands of schools, that allowed students to receive partial credit for work done at a previous school.

It was the sort of policy that was a very big deal for foster kids but that most of the general public knew nothing about. Most people would never have heard about it.

Unless, of course, they happened to be in the company of David Ambroz, as he was breaking the ice by "donating his small talk" and spreading the message about kids in foster care.

CHAPTER SEVEN

ALL BETS ARE OFF

Calling the helpline for problem gamblers, a man in dire circumstances listened to the encouraging words from a volunteer.

But he wasn't buying it.

"You say there's hope," he said to the woman at the other end of the connection. "How would *you* know?"

The hotline operator, Lydia, who was in her seventies, replied simply: "I know because I'm in recovery myself. I'm a gambler."

Until she was forty-three, Lydia had never gambled, other than the occasional bingo game or raffle at the local Catholic church. She had never even bought a lottery ticket.

But on a lark, she took a ride with friends to a nearby casino in Milwaukee, planning on nothing more than spending a few hours of innocent fun. And that would be it.

Sitting at a slot machine, she pulled the lever. Astonishingly, she hit the jackpot. The payout was a whopping $25,000.

"I was unlucky enough," she said, "to get lucky on my first time."

She compared the high of hitting the jackpot to the experience of taking a powerful drug for the first time, the kind of euphoric feeling so powerful that you become driven to recapture it, though as long as you chase, you can never quite reach it.

"It was incredible," she said. "I got the chills. People were cheering for me. It was such a rush."

She chased that rush.

Twenty years earlier, Lydia had found herself divorced and working two jobs to support her children, ages two, three and five.

"We struggled for many, many years," she said.

When the kids were grown, her circumstances eased. She forged a serious relationship with a good man who had a decent job and who would later become her husband. Lydia's own work prospects improved, too. She was able to cut back to one job.

For the first time in her life, she had some discretionary money and some free time.

She would not have imagined that an innocent trip to the casino with friends would be dangerous or life-changing. After the initial big payout, she found herself driving back to the casino to meet friends. When it came time for them to leave, she stayed behind at the slot machine.

Before long, she started going to the casino alone.

As her trips to the gambling parlor became more frequent, she stopped telling her husband where she was going. She would disappear for hours, saying that she had been visiting a friend, or she had gone shopping, though it seemed odd that she never brought anything home from a store.

"I lied so much that even I almost believed what I was saying," she said.

She spent so much time at the casino that she became acquainted with a couple of the floor walkers.

"Have you been here all this time?" one of them asked with a worried tone.

"Oh, I left and came back," she lied.

"Maybe you should go home," the casino worker urged her.

"I will," Lydia told the worker, "in just a little bit."

Lydia's husband was a hunter who spent a week in the North Woods of Wisconsin every November during deer season. The trip gave her an opportunity to visit the casino for seven days straight, and gamble for as long as she wished, without having to explain to anyone where she was going or what she was doing.

When he prepared to leave for hunting, the adrenaline would rush through Lydia, hyped to get back to the slots.

"He would pack up his truck on Thursdays, and I would actually help him, just so that he would leave earlier," she said. "And when he left, I'd give him a head start of ten minutes or so, because he's a slow driver and I didn't want to pass him on the expressway."

She once arrived at the casino at eleven o'clock on a Sunday morning and returned home at eight o'clock the next morning. Through the night, her husband was beside himself. He called her kids. He called the hospitals. He was afraid that she was dead.

"I thought you were having an affair," he would later tell her. "And when I found out what was really going on, I almost *wished* you were having an affair. I could fight another man. I could not fight the casino."

Lydia and her husband each had their own bank account, as well as a shared account. She regularly spent all of her paycheck at the slots, and then went through her personal checking account. Eventually, her gambling ate into the account she shared with her husband, too.

Broke but determined to keep gambling, she "borrowed" a few thousand dollars from her employer, intending to pay it back when her fortunes at the slots took a turn for the better.

Instead, she was caught and charged with theft. She was sentenced to three years of probation and ordered to pay restitution.

"I have a felony on my record," she said. "I am not proud of it. But it is a fact."

Even that did not stop her from gambling.

The moment of reckoning finally came when her husband threatened to divorce her.

"He had every reason to kick me to the curb," she said. "I looked in the mirror and I didn't like who I saw. I had always been an honest person. But the addiction made me do things that were completely out of my character."

She called the Wisconsin Council on Problem Gambling. They urged her to attend a meeting of Gamblers Anonymous.

When she began attending the meetings, the stories she heard from other gamblers hit home. She finally committed to stop gambling. It had taken several years to reach that point. And it had cost her and her husband "hundreds and thousands of dollars" in losses.

"My husband forgave me," she said. "And he's my biggest supporter. But he did *not* forget. And he *will* not forget."

At one of the meetings of Gamblers Anonymous, a plea went out for more volunteers to take calls on the helpline. Lydia went to the meetings faithfully, but she had never worked the hotline.

"You're going to volunteer for that," her sponsor informed her, more *telling* Lydia than *asking* her.

Lydia told her she didn't have the time.

"Make time," the sponsor told her. "It's going to be part of your Twelve-Step program."

She was on call every Friday at five o'clock in the evening until Monday at eight o'clock in the morning. She also worked a sixteen-hour shift every other Monday and Thursday. In an average month, she volunteered 263 hours—a workload far greater than for someone working a full-time job.

On top of that, she led two meetings a week for Gamblers Anonymous. If someone said they could not attend a meeting because it didn't work with their schedule, Lydia would simply create a new meeting with a time that *did* fit their schedule.

It was very difficult to come up with any excuse that would pass muster with Lydia.

Twenty-one years had passed since Lydia stopped gambling and more than sixteen years since she had been volunteering to help those struggling with the problem.

When the phone rang at three o'clock in the morning on Saturday, Lydia picked up.

Her husband had no complaints. It was a lot less trouble than the gambling.

On the helpline, Lydia had grown familiar with the sound of desperation, the shame, the tears:

I've spent all of my money.
I can't buy Christmas presents for the kids.
I lost my home.
I lost my family.
I want to kill myself.

Compared with people who struggle with substance addiction, Lydia explained, gamblers tended to get into much deeper problems before they finally hit bottom.

"With drugs or alcohol, there are outward signs of a problem that are hard to deny," she said. "But with problem gamblers, you don't see anything on the surface, so they can hide it longer."

For those who were not yet ready to acknowledge a problem, Lydia would ask if they were spending more money on gambling than they should be spending.

"Is money that should be going to bills being spent on gambling?"

"Not yet," one caller said.

"The key word is *yet*," Lydia replied.

When a caller talked about suicide, Lydia would respond: "That's a permanent solution to a temporary problem. Everything is fixable."

Lydia and others who worked the phones were instructed to ask such a caller if he or she had a plan in mind about taking their life.

If so, the hotline volunteer was instructed to notify the state Council on Problem Gambling. The council would trace the number and notify the local authorities about the threat.

The phone counselors told callers about the nearby Gamblers Anonymous meetings and contact information for financial experts who could give them advice about their money mess and credit issues. They would send pamphlets and brochures about gambling addiction.

"I'm a bad person," some callers would tell Lydia.

"You're not a bad person," Lydia replied. "Sometimes we make bad choices."

A central theme in Lydia's message was the conviction that no one should feel shame or embarrassment about a gambling problem.

"We had a fellow come to his first meeting last week. He was twenty-seven. He cried like a baby and then he apologized. I told him, 'Don't apologize. Nobody judges you in Gamblers Anonymous. We're all in the same boat.'"

In 2022, Lydia was named as the recipient of the Cornerstone Foundation award as the top volunteer for the Council on Problem Gambling.

Diana Abelt, the group's executive director, described Lydia as a "true blessing" to the organization and to the thousands of people she has helped.

As Lydia saw it, her volunteer work was really a gift for her.

"It's kept me clean."

CHAPTER EIGHT

NOT ACTING HIS AGE

At the age of nineteen, Kevin Soucie left the University of Wisconsin–Madison after his freshman year because he had a wild idea about running for representative in the state legislature.

It was 1974, the Watergate era, and Kevin's childhood neighborhood—a working-class Democratic district in Milwaukee—was filled largely with firefighters, cops and teachers.

Kevin was smart enough to know they might dismiss him as a kid with a crazy dream. As it turned out, they were receptive to his message of openness to new ideas. In the era of scandal in Washington and tragedy in Vietnam, they liked the idea of bringing "new blood" to politics, especially when it was coming from a respectful, soft-spoken local boy.

It didn't hurt that a few years earlier, Kevin had been a standout on the local Hamilton High School basketball team that had won a thrilling state championship.

Kevin won the election. At age twenty, he took the oath of office.

He would serve three terms but eventually decided he should probably go back to the classroom and earn a college degree.

He moved to Montreal and enrolled at McGill University, where he won a starting spot on the school's basketball team—at the relatively old age of twenty-eight.

"After being a serious person at such a young age," he said, "I felt like I was recapturing my youth."

It was in keeping with an offbeat sense of timing that Kevin, as a retired railroad industry executive with grown children and a divorce far in the rearview mirror, would apply to become a volunteer with the Peace Corps—at age sixty-five.

In his application essay, he explained:

> *I suppose I could kick back and watch sunsets and take wonderful excursions around the world (something I still intend to do). But while I would be pursuing those pleasures, I would also be thinking that there are people in the world, especially children, who have little or nothing and can only dream about a life like mine. It's not fair that I was lucky enough to be born an American with all the opportunities and they were not. At this stage of my life, I now want to at least try in some small way to help bring hope to a few people who have little.*

He added:

> *I know there will be days when I will seriously question my sanity for choosing this service when I could be comfortable at home, golfing and sipping margaritas. I know this job won't be easy. But as they say, if it were easy, anybody could do it.*

In an informational packet, the Peace Corps had issued a warning that underscored the hardships.

"It is common for volunteers to use squat toilets, ambulate for miles on uneven terrain, haul water over some distance, and sleep on bedding that does not meet typical U.S. comfort standards."

If he were to be selected, he would be headed to a rugged, remote and impoverished region in the West African nation of Senegal.

The screening process was long and arduous. He was required to submit to a long list of physical tests and bloodwork. He needed doctors to sign off on some twenty documents that attested to his fitness, top to bottom, from dental health to psychological stability.

"You'd think I was applying to be an astronaut at NASA," said Kevin.

Ultimately, he was selected by the Peace Corps, the volunteer program with a mission to provide social assistance around the world, as well as spread goodwill in the name of the United States. The army of peace, as it had been dubbed, was established in 1961 by the executive order of President John F. Kennedy, with a goal of countering the stereotype of the "Ugly American" and "Yankee imperialism."

"It's in our self-interest," Kevin explained. "We can't just take care of America and think we're out of the woods. *We live in the woods.*"

Kevin had been inspired by his father, Donald, a school teacher who had contracted polio at a young age that left him with a slight limp but would not stop him from becoming a Golden Gloves boxer, and his mother, Joan, who "held things together at home," managing a household of six children on a modest budget.

It was part of the Soucie family credo to be grateful for what they had and to rise to the duty to do good works.

"My parents were great Kennedy supporters," Kevin said, "and in our family culture it was important to be involved in the community in ways that would better people's lives."

When the time came for his Peace Corps duty to begin, Kevin and the others in his unit, sixty-eight volunteers—the vast majority of them in their twenties—were called to Philadelphia for a briefing of details about the journey and mission ahead. The meeting served as a sort of gut check for those who might be having second thoughts.

"This is your last chance!" the Peace Corps official called out. "If you're not committed, this is the time to *not* get on the plane!"

No one backed out.

They were bused to LaGuardia Airport, and then boarded a flight headed to Casablanca, where they changed to a plane bound for Dakar, and finally made their way to their remote destination.

The Senegalese families were housed in spartan cinder block buildings, but spent most of their time outside under the trees. They were given nets to guard against mosquitoes, the vectors of the plague of malaria. But the little tents were a hassle to assemble and worsened the heat that regularly soared beyond the 100-degree mark. Many people did not use them.

Kevin and the other volunteers were given a litany of vaccinations, and were required to take a pill each day to guard against malaria.

The volunteers were assigned to the role of health workers, promoting hygiene routines, such as frequent handwashing, which were said to reduce childhood illnesses by one-third, and accompany the Senegalese people to distant, rudimentary clinics, known as health posts. Reaching these health centers required traveling by donkey carts over muddy roads under a blazing sun.

A central part of the mission was to integrate in ways that would build trust and constructive relationships.

Since his college days, Kevin had spoken passable French, one of the languages used in Senegal. To be most effective in his assignment, however, he would need to learn Mandinka.

In Senegal, a Muslim country, gender roles were strictly drawn. The women volunteers were warned not to seem overly friendly—"too available"—and risk sending the wrong message to men. Homosexuality was against the law.

Such views were anathema to the Peace Corps volunteers, some of whom were gay themselves. But Kevin said it was important to bear in mind that, as Americans, they were visitors in a different culture.

"We Americans come in with our modern sensibilities," Kevin said. "But we are their guests. I didn't know much about Islam before I went there. I learned that the faith is very peaceful-minded and family-oriented."

Kevin and the other volunteers were each assigned to live with a family, and the Peace Corps provided money to pay rent for the lodging.

His "host dad" was ten years younger than Kevin. His name was Lamine Sagna and he served as the village chief. While the men were allowed to take up to seven wives, he had only one.

A man who radiated kindness, Lamine regarded Kevin as a family member and bestowed upon him the name Mamadou Sagna.

"What a great man," Kevin said of his "dad," the village chief. "He had never gone to school a day in his life, but he could speak six languages. And he was willing to take me to anyone I needed to meet. He was a real schmoozer."

The Senegalese survived economically largely through growing cashews and fishing, a difficult living.

"It's a tough go," Kevin said. "That's why you have a lot of people getting into those little boats and trying to sail to Italy."

Kevin would shower and wash his clothes by scooping water out of a bucket he kept in his room. He was hesitant to draw water from the well outside, he said, because girls or women would quickly appear and insist that it was their duty to do such a chore for a man. He did not want to take advantage of them, but neither did he want to offend.

The children, meanwhile, would follow Kevin with a chair wherever he walked (he was considered an elder, after all, being in his mid-sixties), ready to assist him if he chose to sit down. He expressed honor for the culture's deep respect for older people, like him, but noted that he certainly did not request or require any such coddling.

Kevin said the young Senegalese exuded extraordinary warmth. They would rush alongside him, drawing close to hold his hand and talk cheerfully. When he sat down, they would affectionately drape their arms around his shoulders.

He delighted in watching the kids at play, mostly kicking a ball around. Seeing people with so little in material terms who found such joy in life, he said, was a useful lesson for an American.

"Even though people are poor, it doesn't mean they are unhappy," he said. "In fact, I'd never seen so many happy children in my life."

When Kevin would retreat to his room to read or write, people would often grow concerned. The Senegalese were a very social people, and worried that his need for solitude might signal that something was wrong.

"We Americans love our individualism and privacy," he said. "A Senegalese person doesn't know why anyone would want to be alone."

At the health center, Kevin met with the midwife, whose position was especially highly respected.

"She was my go-to person," he said.

Kevin observed that many villagers would make long trips to the health center, only to find that the aide they hoped to meet was not around.

He came up with an idea to establish a scheduling and phone system that would help the system run more efficiently. But it was vital that any change in the custom not be seen as imposed by an outsider. He partnered with the midwife on the initiative, deferring to her on the proposal. She invited him to join her in making a presentation about the plan to a group gathered at the health post. People listened and expressed a consensus in favor of the plan.

One of the goals of the health post was the promotion of contraceptives. Girls in Senegal were often married and pregnant at thirteen. The midwife told Kevin that she had encountered a pregnant girl who was only eleven.

During his time in Senegal, both of Kevin's parents died.

"It was a helpless feeling," he said, being so far away.

He had tried to make his way home when he learned that his mother had fallen seriously ill.

"I was in a car racing to Dakar when I got word from my daughter that it was too late," he said.

Not long afterwards, his father passed away.

It gave him some comfort to know that he was carrying out the kind of work that they had encouraged him to do since he was a child.

Thirteen months into Kevin's service, the COVID-19 pandemic terrorized the world, and every Peace Corps volunteer was called back home.

"I was so disappointed," he said. "I understand why the Peace Corps did it. On the other hand, we were recruited to a country with a long list of diseases, some of which are far worse than COVID-19."

Though it came to an end too soon, working as a Peace Corps volunteer was one of the most meaningful experiences of his life.

He had grown deeply fond of the Senegalese people. And he was heartened by the selflessness of the American volunteers in his group, young people who were surely surprised to see a sixty-five-year-old man tromping around.

"I never felt excluded," he said, "but neither did I try to be one of them."

Back in the United States, he kept in touch with many of his old volunteer partners.

"It was a special time," he said. "You've got this shared experience under very challenging conditions. You are isolated in so many ways—language, geography, culture.

"This is a good experience, not a complaint."

In an American society where so many people were searching for a purpose, and a way to change the world, Kevin became a booster of the Peace Corps experience to people of his age.

"I'm surprised there aren't more older people joining the Peace Corps," he said. "We've got a lot of boomers retiring with the time and desire to do something meaningful."

Back home in his apartment in Milwaukee, Kevin talked at least once a week on the phone with his host father, the village chief.

He played a recent message, listening as the man was asking about Kevin's son.

The message from his "dad" in Senegal made Kevin smile. He was grateful for their enduring bond.

CHAPTER NINE

UNTIL THE END

Judy Goldthorp felt some anxiety as she rang the doorbell. She was about to meet a person who was dying.

"You've been given a name and some basic information," she said. "But you really don't know what to expect."

The door opened and she stepped inside, ready to do whatever was needed—helping people she had never met, in a moment when they were so very fragile.

As a volunteer for hospice, Judy devoted her time and energy to easing the last journey for dying patients, and lending warmth and support to their loved ones.

She would sit at the bedside of the dying, holding a hand, leaning in to comprehend some whispered words. She listened to fond memories and maybe some sorrows. She fetched food and drinks, shared in watching a favorite television show, listened to a special song, read aloud from a beloved book. She trailed behind patients who were unsteady on their feet. She held a fork and spoon to feed them. She combed their hair, washed their bodies, changed their diapers.

"The thing about hospice," as Judy put it, "is that ordinary people do extraordinary things."

For the family members, too, volunteers like Judy offered support, guidance and encouragement. In some cases, they carefully navigated the minefield of family tensions in times that could be emotionally charged.

They ran errands to the store, or they stayed back with the patient, giving loved ones a break—a chance to step outside, take a ride, go home for a nap, and perhaps take some time to weep in private.

When she retired from nursing, Judy, a Texan in her seventies, had not planned on volunteering for hospice.

But then came a call.

"Can you help?"

It was supposed to be a one-time incident.

Before long, Judy was receiving about twenty-five calls or emails a week.

"I have a hard time saying no," she said.

For Judy, it became virtually a full-time job, without pay or benefits, but with rewards in other meaningful ways.

It meant being adaptable. There was the patient in his eighties, a bit on the grumpy side, whose favorite pastime was watching old Westerns on television.

"So at one o'clock we would turn on *Gunsmoke*," she said, "and after that it was *Hopalong Cassidy*."

There was the patient whose bedroom walls were covered with artwork of local Texas scenes. They had been painted by his late wife, he explained, and having them nearby made him feel that she was close to him.

There was the patient who asked to be taken to the local places she had long visited in her everyday routine.

"She knew everybody at Whole Foods," said Judy. "She knew all of the people at the post office. She knew the workers at Kroger's."

She might not have even needed to buy anything. But the dying woman knew the day was coming when she would no longer be able to rise from her bed and see the familiar faces.

And that day would come soon.

There was the patient who watched cable news and uttered commentary on all sorts of subjects, often tinged with harsh opinions.

"Have you ever thought of it this way?" Judy once asked.

The woman quickly cut her off.

"I didn't say anything about her comments after that," she said. "As a hospice volunteer, you have to remember that this is their home and you are a guest."

The families of the patients, meanwhile, were often exhausted, emotionally raw, and sometimes left questioning the wisdom of their own decisions.

"In some cases, they're barely able to hold it together," Judy said. "They're feeling under pressure; they're so worried about doing something the wrong way."

And then there were complicated family dynamics.

Judy cared for a dying woman who lived by herself in an apartment. A daughter would sometimes come to visit, but the two of them could never seem to get along.

"I was the go-between," said Judy, who would relay the "concerns" that mother or daughter had expressed.

Rarely would either of them budge.

"Yeah," the daughter once remarked about her mother's perspective, "that's what her ninety-two-year-old self *would* say."

Judy thought to herself:

"It's not for me to say, 'Be nicer to your mother,'" she said. "It's not my mother and I haven't walked that path."

But she did suggest to the daughter that rather than continue to rehash their longstanding differences, she might just "give her a hug."

She did, and the embrace seemed to soften both of them.

Judy was not attending the elderly woman when she died, but she got word about her death from hospice.

She had made it a point to try to attend funerals. It brought her closure, and it meant a lot to the families.

Hospice did not inform volunteers about services after a death, so she scanned the obituaries in search of information about the woman's services, and found an address for the graveside ceremony.

"At the cemetery," she said, "I went from green tent to green tent."

She finally found the right place. At the gravesite, there was only the daughter and a friend, who played "Taps," a tribute to the mother's service in World War II.

During the time spent together, Judy and the daughter had forged a connection that grew into a friendship that endured long afterward.

"She's a very interesting person," Judy said. "She knows stuff I wouldn't even think to ask about."

Not all hospice volunteers worked at the bedside. Volunteers also cared for a family pet, babysat, picked up children from school, or shuttled them to sports practice or games. There were volunteers who did clerical work, and those with special skills—barbers, beauticians, groundskeepers, musicians—who contributed their gifts to comfort.

In working with the dying, it had been Judy's experience, most of the caregiving was done by women in the family, though not always.

"One of the best caretakers I've ever seen was a husband whose wife had ALS," a fatal illness commonly known as Lou Gehrig's disease. "I still think about him. He was amazing. He would do anything. He would dress her bedsores."

It was not uncommon for differences about care to arise within the family, especially when one or more of the children was living distantly—and swooped in from far away to raise objections.

"Hospice workers in Texas refer to that as the 'Daughter from California,'" she said. "In other places, I hear they call it the 'Daughter from Texas.'"

For someone who hasn't been around to see the decline, Judy said, it could be difficult to understand and accept.

The last they knew, she said, the mother was feeling cheerful and was up and around, telling stories and cooking dinner.

They understandably didn't want to lose that person. But the person they remembered, in important ways, was often already gone.

"Why are we doing hospice care? Mom should be in the hospital!"

Meanwhile the local daughter is in the kitchen, Judy said, "banging her head against the wall and thinking, 'Where were you when I needed you?'"

In some cases, Judy would step in and make a gentle suggestion.

"Why don't we ask Mom?" she would say. "And Mom would usually say, 'I want to stay at home.'"

Besides visiting the homes of the dying, Judy called to check on them.

"I called a man the other day and I asked, 'What do you need?'

"And he answered, 'Dog food. I need dog food.' And so I went to the store and got dog food."

A common concern among family members focused on the use of painkillers, usually morphine. They didn't want a loved one to suffer in pain, but they feared it might hasten death.

"What you're doing is right," she would tell family members who felt guilty about giving the drugs. "Focus on comfort. Families need to hear that over and over."

Sometimes, she would ask a daughter or son: "What would you want for yourself?"

The answer usually came easily. No one really wanted to linger in terrible pain.

In many cases, family members simply need a break.

"They'll say, 'I just need to run to the store,'" Judy said. "And I'll tell them, 'You don't have to run.'"

Judy knew from her own experience about the burdens of caring for a loved one. When she took care of her mother, after a hip surgery, she recalled the feeling of being confined for long stretches.

When her mother needed her to pick up some prescription drugs, Judy acknowledged feeling a welcome sense of freedom in leaving the house and going to the supermarket.

"I walked all over the store, *just because I could*," she said. "I know what it's like to be isolated."

Years later, when her mother lay in a hospital, undergoing treatment for heart failure that had reached the end stage, Judy asked gently:

"Do you want to go home for hospice?"

"Yes," her mother said without hesitation.

"I can make that happen," the daughter told her.

And she did.

"My mother was ninety-three," Judy said, "and she had been giving people hell until probably the last six weeks of her life."

On April 5, 2007, her mother's time came.

"It was just Mom and me," said Judy.

Since then, Judy has helped countless patients and families get through to the end, drawing on goodwill and kindness.

"When people talk about the world going to hell in a handbasket," she said, "I think about my hospice people."

CHAPTER TEN

AN ANCESTOR'S WHISPER

Still behind the steering wheel at ninety-two, Joan Southgate zipped around the East Side of Cleveland in her old Toyota Echo, before stopping for a ginger ale at one of her favorite haunts, Hell's Fried Chicken.

It was a brief pit stop.

A four-foot-eight-inch dynamo ("I was once four-eleven," she noted, just for the record), she was in a hurry to get to the historic Cozad-Bates House in the city's arts district.

She had successfully fought to save the old Bates building from the wrecking ball. It was now the home of a center on the Underground Railroad, the network of clandestine routes and safe houses for enslaved Black people escaping bondage in the mid-1800s.

Outside the building, a plaque had just been installed: "Joan Evelyn Southgate Walk."

It honored Joan's dedication to saving the building, once the home of committed abolitionists, and pushing for a center that focused on the local history of Black liberation.

"She led the charge," said Chris Ronayne, the president of University Circle, an arts and museum district, which oversaw the Cozad-Bates House and the Underground Railroad exhibit. "She is our conscience."

Widely regarded as a godmother of community activism in this city, Joan powered forward on this crisp spring morning in her blue and orange sneakers, clutching a wooden cane.

In her long history as a civic volunteer for social causes, her list of crusades included leading demonstrations to demand better access to pharmacies for the elderly, scaling a fence to protest a nuclear power plant, saving the historic Cozad-Bates House, and taking a very long walk to remind young people—and many who were not so young—about the history of the Underground Railroad.

Joan walked the route of the Underground Railroad, staying in homes along the way, to honor the runaway enslaved people and those who aided them. She had stepped off her journey in Ripley, Ohio, south of Cincinnati, and made her way to Pennsylvania, New York, and finally to Canada, where so many of those who were fleeing shackles would ultimately find freedom.

It was hardly the typical outing for a woman who was then in her mid-seventies.

"I'm sure a lot of people were wondering, 'What in the world is this little old Black lady doing?'"

As Joan proudly noted, Ohio boasted more stops on the Underground Railroad than any other state. Among the enslaved people trying to escape to freedom, she said, Cleveland was known, in code speak, as "Hope."

For that reason, Joan and her allies chose "Restore Cleveland Hope" as the name for a movement to organize an interpretive exhibit and teaching center at Cozad-Bates.

The idea for a way to honor those in the Underground Railroad came to her on a morning walk in her Cleveland neighborhood.

"Who were those amazing people?" she had wondered then, and later wrote. "How could they do it? Taking children. Small babes slung across their hips… what was it like and how could I praise them? The answer fell into place as I rounded the corner for home. An ancestor's whisper: 'Walk.'"

She had grown up in Syracuse, in upstate New York. She was one of the very few Black students of her time to attend Syracuse University.

The region had been a hotbed of the abolition and women's suffrage movements. Her mother, Evelyn Claracy Harris, had grown up in Auburn, New York, the small town that was also the home of Harriet Tubman, who escaped slavery in the South and led some thirteen missions to rescue an estimated seventy enslaved people, using the network of safe houses along the Underground Railroad.

A photograph of Harriet Tubman, taken in her later years, had been handed down to Joan from her mother and now occupied a sacred place in the Southgate home.

When Joan shared her idea for the long walk, some people cautioned against it.

"You could get hurt," warned a neighbor.

She said others just smiled and remarked, "Oh, that's Joan."

Family members and close friends were behind her from the start. They organized to help, doing research on the route of the Underground Railroad, sending emails and snail mail to people who might be willing to offer a place for Joan to stay for a night along her way.

Walking an average of ten miles a day, Joan stayed in the homes of supportive strangers who were delighted to learn more about the history from this remarkable older woman.

She went to schools, churches and city council meetings to give talks about the Underground Railroad and answer questions from the curious residents about her mission.

"I wanted them to know why I was doing it and to raise awareness that conductors were white and Black, and that they were the civil rights activists of the time."

She tried to explain to children how difficult the escape had been for kids. For long, long stretches, they had to stay silent. Or they would arouse suspicion that could lead to arrest and a return to slavery.

"Just try to *imagine* the stress," she told them.

She would ask the classroom to remain absolutely silent for a whole minute—it wasn't easy—and then for two minutes.

It was usually impossible.

Just think, Joan told the kids, about the runaway children who needed to stay silent for an hour or even longer.

That got through.

Joan stressed that the conductors, who were typically white, were also courageous. Although Ohio was a free state, the Fugitive Slave Law of 1850 made it a crime to help runaway slaves. The law required that all slaves be returned to their masters. People who aided fugitive slaves could lose their property, be fined up to $1,000, and go to jail.

Toward the end of Joan's journey, as she approached the border of Canada, she held hands with her daughter, Teci, and her seven-year-old granddaughter, Helena, who had come to join her for the last triumphant steps.

Together, they walked across Peace Bridge, then ran to meet family and friends who had traveled to the destination to congratulate Joan, cheering as their cameras were clicking.

In a slight drizzle, Joan and her supporters walked the last few miles to Salem Chapel, a church founded by freedom seekers in St. Catharines, Ontario. The most celebrated member of the church congregation was Harriet Tubman, often called Moses, who had moved to Canada after Congress passed the Fugitive Slave Act.

When Joan saw the church, she broke into a smile and ran to the stairs of Salem Chapel. Throngs of people were waiting and cheering, including the mayor of the town.

At the top of the stairs, a Black man played a harmonica to greet her. Two little girls placed bouquets of wildflowers in her arms.

The 2002 journey would culminate in a book she authored, *In Their Path: A Grandmother's 519-Mile Underground Railroad Walk*, and ultimately, a center to commemorate the nineteenth century movement.

Inside the old refurbished brick Cozad-Bates building, posters and panels now recount Cleveland's proud role in the anti-slavery movement, as well as some of the indignities suffered by Black people, in those days and for many years afterward.

"My wrists were tied crosswise together, and my hands were brought down and tied to my ankles," read the words on a panel from John Malvin, who wrote about the brutality of his years in bondage.

"My shirt was taken off, and in that condition, I was compelled to lie on the ground, and he began flogging me. He whipped me on the one side until the flesh was all raw and bleeding, then he rolled me over like a log and whipped on the other side."

As printed materials in the exhibit explained, those who reached Cleveland were hidden, housed and fed by local abolitionists before being assisted to the port at Lake Erie, where they would climb into a boat bound for Canada—a free country whose code name among those seeking liberty was "God Be Praised."

The walls of the exhibit were covered with replicas of the abolitionist posters of the era.

"Fugitive Slaves Attention! The slave hunter is among us! Be on your guard! An arrest is planned for tonight!"

Another banner called to white people of conscience:

"Turn out and learn your duty to yourselves, the slave and God!"

The exhibit paid tribute to William Howard Day, editor of the first Black newspaper in Cleveland, as well as Robert Leach, the first African American physician in the city.

But resistance to the Underground Railroad was strong, too. As one exhibit detailed, the *Cleveland Plain Dealer*, still the dominant newspaper in the city, ran editorials in favor of the Fugitive Slave Act, a safeguard against the city coming to resemble "the Congo."

In her two-story blue house, Joan sat at the dining room table with a cup of tea, a green shawl draped around her shoulders. She was using hearing aids these days, and she observed that, "Lately, I'm having a little problem finding nouns."

But her eyes still sparkled behind large oval frames, and her thirst for social justice had scarcely been quenched.

A portrait of the comedian and activist Dick Gregory stared out from the wall, near a rendering of Malcolm X. Elsewhere in her home, a drawing depicted Black people in chains at the beginning and, at last, a triumphant Barack Obama. In between were figures that powered the movement in civil rights—the celebrated orator Frederick Douglass, Supreme Court Justice Thurgood Marshall, writer Phillis Wheatley, abolitionist Harriet Tubman, Congressional representative Shirley Chisholm, civil rights leaders Medgar Evers and Dr. Martin Luther King Jr.

Joan's husband, Robert Southgate, a teacher who became a librarian, had died many years earlier. The couple had first met at the Karamu House, the first integrated theater in Cleveland, where they had both worked as volunteers. She was doing props and he was doing sound for Eugène Labiche's nineteenth-century farce, *The Italian Straw Hat*.

A retired social worker, Joan had earned a master's degree at Case Western Reserve University in Cleveland. In her early years, she had worked with foster children in Brooklyn, where she lived in a three-story walk-up.

She could still recall placing a mixed-race child with white parents, only to receive a telephone call after a month, saying they wished to return the baby because she was "too dark."

"She was beautiful," Joan remembered.

For Joan, the appreciation of diversity was no mere slogan. It was her life.

"My family has it all: Christian, Jew and Muslim; tall and short; gay and straight; fat and thin; rich and poor; Black, white and Latino."

She said her belief in the innate goodness of people, no matter their background, was rewarded again and again during her walk on the path of the Underground Railroad.

She would never forget a trucker named Al, a towering white man who stopped near her suddenly on a desolate highway in rural Ohio. He had read about her walk in a local newspaper.

"Mrs. Southgate?" he asked, as he stepped down from his big rig.

She nodded hesitantly, not knowing what to expect.

"I just had to stop and say thank you," he said, breaking out in a broad smile. "What you are doing is grand."

And then he pulled out the newspaper with the article about her journey.

He asked her to autograph it for his children.

CHAPTER ELEVEN

WHENEVER THE CALL COMES

When the phone rang for Bill Ledford, a Nevadan in his sixties, he might have been shopping, or having dinner with a friend, or deep in sleep. The call might have come at seven o'clock in the evening or three o'clock in the morning. No matter the hour, he rushed out to help.

Someone he had never met needed Bill's support in a terrifying time. He worked as a volunteer for survivors of sexual assault.

"I'm Bill and I'm your advocate," he would introduce himself at the clinic. "I am so sorry this happened to you."

His mission focused on how he could help: whether it was securing the morning-after pill or medicine for a sexually transmitted disease, getting contact information for a counselor or psychologist, or finding out about financial assistance for lost wages or medical treatment.

More than anything else, however, it was his job to convey a single, vital truth:

This was not your fault.

In more than a decade of advocating for sexual assault survivors, he had grown accustomed to hearing self-blame:

I was dressed like a slut.

I had been drinking.

I shouldn't have gone to the party.

Bill told the survivors they were entitled to dress however they wanted, entitled to drink, entitled to go to a bar or a party—without being assaulted.

"Nobody," he stressed, "asks to be raped."

He would inquire gently:

"Can you tell me what he did to you?"

Like other advocates, Bill would bring a stuffed animal for the survivor to clutch.

"When someone is in a bad way," he explained, "they want to hold something for comfort."

There were a range of reactions among the survivors.

"Sometimes they're crying. Sometimes they want a hug. Sometimes they want distance."

A native of Monmouth, New Jersey, Bill had moved to Sparks, Nevada, to take a job at a casino as a surveillance agent, on the lookout for theft and fraud by customers or employees.

His yearning to volunteer, he said, grew out of a desire to fill a void after going through a divorce.

In his younger days, he had found volunteering to be meaningful and gratifying. At age fifteen, he had worked as a volunteer on the local First Aid squad, as a cadet. Mostly, he delivered minor assistance, such as applying bandages to a kid who had been scraped while playing. But some cases were more serious. At age seventeen, he helped with an emergency delivery of a baby. At eighteen, he performed CPR, cardiopulmonary resuscitation, on an elderly man who had suffered a heart attack.

"It was scary," he recalled. "Sitting in the classroom during training and visualizing it is one thing. But when you're with a live person, it gives you a totally different perspective."

In college at Glassboro State College, now Rowan University, Bill volunteered to work with a probation officer. The assignments mostly involved talking with young people who had gotten caught up in shoplifting, auto theft, drug use, or consumption of alcohol as a minor.

In some cases, the young truants would scoff that they didn't need any of his help.

"I'm only doing this because the probation officer said I had to," one young tough scoffed, insisting that no one really cared about him anyway.

"I'm *here* for you," Bill told him. "I'm not getting paid. I'm here because I want to help you. Maybe you had a bad home life growing up. But there are other ways to go from here. I care about you and I want you to get your life back on track. And I don't even know you."

That seemed to surprise the teenager—and it clicked. By the end of the counseling sessions, he told Bill he was genuinely grateful and vowed to try his best to adopt a new attitude and stay clear of trouble.

Bill said he might have inherited the ethic for volunteering from his parents. His father had served on the city council, as well as the school board, and coached Pop Warner youth football. His mother helped elderly people prepare their taxes, at no charge.

When he arrived in Nevada, Bill searched the ads for volunteer opportunities and reached out to a place called, simply, Crisis Center. He made clear that he would work in any capacity needed. He received a call back from a supervisor who asked if he would be willing to work nights.

Bill agreed.

Would he be willing to work with survivors of sexual assault?

Initially, Bill was a bit puzzled.

"For a woman who has just been sexually assaulted," he asked the supervisor, "is the first thing she wants to see some strange man?"

The supervisor explained that survivors of sexual assault had been given the choice. Did they prefer a man or a woman as an advocate? Did it matter?

"Think of it this way," he told Bill. "It might be a way to show a woman in that situation that there really *are* some good men out there."

He also explained that while women were most likely to be targeted for sexual assault, some men had been assaulted, too, especially those who were gay or transgender.

The training for sexual assault advocacy consisted of fifteen hours a week for six to eight weeks. The sessions included mock interviews, where the trainees were taught how to gather information and relay assistance. They were advised to encourage the survivors to keep a journal, so they could "get their thoughts out of their head and on to paper." And they were told to emphasize to survivors that they had done nothing wrong. They did not "ask for it."

In the case of gay and trans survivors, Bill would come to learn, it was not uncommon for additional abuse to be heaped on the survivors by the very medical workers who treated them for the assault, belittling them for being "weird."

Sex workers who had been attacked, meanwhile, male and female, often were reluctant to file a report of an assault with the police because they feared being locked up themselves. And then there were children who were assaulted, often by a family member.

As an advocate, Bill would follow up weekly, and then monthly, for as long as the survivor wished. In some cases, he would stay in contact for as long as two years.

As time passed, he would grow optimistic that a survivor was healing. He began to detect a change in the tone of their voice. He would ask how they were doing. Had they gone back to work? From the first interaction, he assured the survivor that anything said to an advocate remained confidential.

The exchanges have been good for both the survivor and the advocate.

"It's made me a better person," Bill said, "knowing I can help someone get back on their feet."

Bill logged so many hours in one recent year—1,800—that he was named the Northern Nevada Volunteer of the Year.

He has taken calls that disrupted plans when he was visiting with his two sons. He has walked out of a movie when he was needed. He has spent the entire night with a survivor, and then gone to work exhausted.

"Sometimes, there's just not time to sleep," he said.

He had been fortunate to have a supportive manager at work. Many times, the boss had told him—as long as there was a second person on the floor doing surveillance—he could go ahead and leave work to meet with a survivor.

That wasn't always the case at home. Bill remarried, but his second wife often objected to his devotion to his volunteer work.

"When we were sitting at home, and I would get a call to go out, she would resent it," he said. "I let her know, 'This is what I do—this is who I am.'"

They ultimately divorced.

Sometimes, finances have been tight for Bill. With all of the hours he has spent volunteering, he knew he could have taken a second job, even a third, to bring in more income.

"But there was more of a payout," he said, "in helping other people."

CHAPTER TWELVE

NO SOLDIER'S FAMILY LEFT BEHIND

Raised in a patriotic, blue-collar family in Massachusetts, George MacClary graduated from high school in 1967 and promptly joined the United States Marines Corps to fight the war in Vietnam.

"I felt the country was trying to stop communism," he said, "and I wanted to do the right thing."

Not yet old enough to legally drink a beer or cast a vote, he signed up for the infantry, the frontline combat troops fighting enemy forces in a dangerous mountain range not far from Hanoi.

About one year later, his young life nearly came to an end. An exploding grenade ripped through his body and riddled him with shrapnel. He was airlifted from An Hòa to Japan, and then to the Chelsea Navy Hospital in Massachusetts. After a long and painful recovery, George returned to his hometown of Waltham, where he went to work as a firefighter.

He was decorated with a Purple Heart. But like many American veterans of the Vietnam War, he was not exactly treated as a returning hero. Instead, his service was generally greeted with indifference, or worse.

"Not that we expected a parade," he said, "but it was pretty cold out there for Vietnam veterans."

As the years passed, his own view of the war evolved.

"As time goes on and you think of the 58,000 guys who lost their lives, you wonder, 'What was gained?'"

Besides "all those dead," he said, there were the badly wounded—burned, blinded, missing limbs—as well as those suffering with what he described as "the invisible injuries."

George married a schoolteacher, became a father, and rose in the ranks to captain on the fire squad. He watched as a generation and more of men and women went off to fight in subsequent wars, some of them never to return, others to come home and struggle mightily to fit.

"We all watched Iraq and Afghanistan soldiers coming home banged up," he said, enduring physical, emotional and financial troubles. "I hated to see those kids go wanting after having done so much."

Besides the returning soldiers, there were so many spouses and children, too, who faced financial and emotional hardships.

When George retired and moved to Florida with his wife, Joan, in 2010, he decided to do something to help. He approached the board of directors at the modest country club he had joined and asked if he could organize a golf tournament as a fundraiser for injured or fallen vets and their families.

"We're not wealthy people and it's not a fancy club," he said. "We do what we can."

In the first year, the tournament raised $10,000. After ten more years of tournaments, with the help of Joan, and a daughter, Jordan, the fund for vets and families had grown to more than $1 million.

When he looked for a group to distribute the money, George carefully researched organizations that promoted themselves as advocates for military families. He knew that some groups were more reputable than others.

He settled on Hope for the Warriors, an organization founded in 2006 by two military spouses aboard Marine Corps Base Camp Lejeune, North Carolina. Its stated mission was serving "those touched by military service" by helping "to restore a sense of self, family and hope." The group made a special outreach to single-income households and spouses, people whose challenges tended to be overlooked by the military.

One of the beneficiaries of that help was Jennifer McCollum.

Born at Fort Knox, a military base in Kentucky, the daughter of a lieutenant colonel, she spent parts of her childhood in Gelnhausen, Germany, and Fort Hood, Texas, among other places. She was a self-described Army brat.

She studied at Virginia Tech, and later volunteered at a children's hospital in Bucharest, Romania. Many of the kids in the hospital had been abandoned. At twenty-two years old, Jennifer watched a child die. She vowed that she would spend her life caring for young people who needed help.

On September 11, 1999, Jennifer met Dan McCollum, a lieutenant in the Marines, who was just about to begin flight training to become a pilot.

He was smart, handsome and humble, as well as an Eagle Scout, a Black Belt expert, a collegiate wrestler, and a graduate of Clemson University.

When Jennifer described this seemingly too-good-to-be-true young man to her pastor, the preacher asked:

"Does he also ride a white horse?"

Within a year of their dating, Dan rented a small Cessna plane and flew the two of them to pristine Ocracoke Island in North Carolina, where he asked for her hand.

They were married on Memorial Day weekend in 2001, in a chapel at the Marine Corps headquarters in Quantico, Virginia. The newlyweds moved to San Diego, where Dan was stationed.

"All the world was right," as Jennifer put it. "We had a fabulous group of friends. We spent the weekends barbecuing or at the beach. We were all in our mid-twenties. Everything was coming along beautifully."

Jennifer worked in family outreach in foster homes, assessing the development skills and the target goals of the children. Dan taught hand-to-hand combat to Marines at the base. They bought a condo. It seemed that life could not be any better.

And then came 9/11.

"When he came home from work that night, it was absolutely harrowing," she remembered. "Our story of that day was no different than anyone else's in the country."

But their story would quickly change. Two weeks after the terrorist attacks on America, Dan's squadron was called up to deploy. The War on Terror was beginning.

They knew he was going somewhere. Afghanistan? Bahrain? Pakistan?

On the morning of the planned deployment, on September 26, 2001, she sent him on his way with "the biggest bag of trail mix and an entire loaf of ham sandwiches."

Later that day, however, he called Jennifer to tell her he wouldn't be leaving with this wave of troops after all.

Dan came home. Jennifer was relieved. They talked about starting a family.

"I wanted to be a mom, but I decided to wait a year," she said. "Little did we know, I was already pregnant."

Dan was thrilled about the baby.

"He would talk to my stomach," she said. "He'd say, 'Hello in there! What did you do today?'"

"He was already being a good dad."

The first ultrasound was conducted on December 6, 2001. The next day, he would be deployed—this time for real.

Jennifer and Dan tried to focus on the positive. Like pretty much everything else in their life together, they felt certain that it all would work out beautifully. Dan would be back home in March. The baby would be born in June. They had chosen names and decided on the godparents.

"I remember saying out loud, 'I refuse to allow this deployment to be a stressful event,'" Jennifer recalled. "He was going to go and come home and it was going to be great."

In those early days of the U.S. military action, there had been very few American casualties. Boosters of the excursion were predicting the operation would be safe, short and decisive. Jennifer and Dan had good reason to be optimistic. On the day he deployed, she walked him to the tarmac at the San Diego base.

"I'll see you soon," she told him. "Be safe."

Scarcely a month later, on January 9, 2002, Jennifer was driving to a home visit for her foster care job when her cell phone rang. It was a number from work. That was odd, she thought, since they knew she was at an appointment. She would call them later.

And then the phone rang at the house she was visiting. The foster mom picked up, then handed the phone to Jennifer.

"You need to come back to the office," a coworker told her.

"Is everything okay?" Jennifer asked.

The colleague spoke in a calm voice and didn't relay any bad news.

"Oh," Jennifer replied, relieved for an instant, "I was afraid you were going to tell me something was wrong with Dan."

On the other end of the line, there was just enough of a pause to make Jennifer worry.

She got in her car and began driving back to work, switching on the news radio.

In a solemn voice, the radio broadcaster reported that a U.S. Marine plane had crashed in Pakistan.

"I knew," Jennifer said. "I just knew."

And then her phone rang from another Marine's wife who was beside herself with worry, but hadn't received any official notification. And then came a call from another terrified Marine's wife.

"I pulled off the road and parked the car," Jennifer said. "And I sobbed."

She drove back to work and walked into the office. Some of the colleagues scattered. She saw a coworker who was visibly upset.

"Did they call?" Jennifer asked. "Are they coming?"

Yes, the coworker told her, they were coming.

After waiting for what seemed like an eternity, a contingent arrived at the workplace: a chaplain, a commanding officer, and two Marine pilots who were good friends to Dan and Jennifer.

They somberly told her what they knew. The plane had gone down. There had been a fire. Attempts to find any survivors had so far been unsuccessful.

"My main thought was, 'He'll be able to find his way out,'" Jennifer remembered. "I thought that for years. Even after we buried him."

Dan had been the fighter copilot of a C-130 aircraft on a mission in Pakistan. They had been told to fly under the cover of darkness. The pilots were trying to land at a small airstrip between mountains on a moonless night. The left wing of the plane clipped the mountainside and crashed.

Dan was twenty-eight. Jennifer was twenty-seven. On June 11, 2002, their baby boy was born. They had intended to name him David. Instead, Jennifer decided to give him the name Daniel.

"I wanted him to have everything he could have of his father," she explained.

Rather than go back to work right away, she decided to stay home with her son because she believed that was what the boy needed.

"Out of the gate," she said, "he was down one parent."

Her world had turned upside down. She had lost a spouse, her child's father, and a community who shared the Marine life.

Jennifer learned quickly that she and her baby were collateral damage—and that nobody was coming to the rescue.

"The military was not set up to take care of widows," she said. "There were so many gaps and holes in how surviving families were treated."

She reached out to the military repeatedly, to little avail.

"You can only say 'I need help' so many times before you realize you're alone," she said.

Dan had signed up for a modest insurance policy. She was grateful to him, and she was frugal with the money. But times were lean. She was twice denied a refinance of her home because she didn't make enough money.

She knew others were going through the same troubles. To help them cope, she volunteered to tell her story to other military families. She hoped it would help inspire a movement.

"I wanted to be a hand to hold," she said.

She joined a group of military spouses pushing for change in the way survivors were treated. In 2005, she testified before the Veterans Affairs Committee of the U.S. Senate.

"Military spouses need an advocate," she said. "I watched high-ranking officers say everything was all right. It just wasn't true. I wanted to tell people the truth they hadn't heard."

At those hearings, she met a sympathetic young senator from Illinois named Barack Obama. Years later, Jennifer and young Daniel, by then a teenager, would be invited to the White House with other military families to greet President Obama.

With Daniel growing older, Jennifer hoped to enroll in graduate school to earn a master's degree that would allow her to become a certified counselor for children. She filed an application and essay to Hope for the Warriors and was selected for a scholarship.

"It helped me not to be forced to take on more debt," she said. "It plugged a hole that was leaking."

She would earn a master's degree from Liberty University. She landed a job in a school district, working with young people who were experiencing anxiety, depression, and thoughts of suicide.

Daniel would go on to graduate from high school and win acceptance to the esteemed University of North Carolina School of the Arts, with plans to earn a bachelor of fine arts degree in acting.

He had the smarts, talent and handsome looks for the stage or screen.

"He looks just like his father," said Jennifer.

CHAPTER THIRTEEN

A KID'S BEST FRIEND

On a sticky Sunday afternoon during the dog days of summer, Macey made her way into the conference room, arriving well before her clients. She was poised for business.

"She knows she's here to work, not socialize," said Macey's supervisor, Nancy Endow.

To be sure, a disciplined form of socializing was, indeed, part of Macey's job description, so long as she carried herself in a dignified and respectful manner. She knew the rules:

No licking anyone's face. No smelling any behinds.

Macey was a puggle, a mix of pug and beagle. She was a therapy dog who worked with kids growing up with physical and developmental challenges.

Around her neck, Macey wore a rainbow-colored kerchief imprinted with the words, "Special Dogs for Special Kids."

On this day, she would be hanging out with a couple of twelve-year-old boys, each of whom had experienced some struggles, but who felt loved and accepted unconditionally by therapy dogs.

Macey's first playmate of the day was Adrian Phillips, who wore a red Chicago Bulls t-shirt. He was just about to enter the sixth grade. When he was younger, he was scared of dogs and all other animals, too.

But now, after working with therapy dogs for a handful of years, pups were his best friends.

When he saw Macey, he dropped to the floor so he could be at eye level with the dog, and within easy reach of a touch.

"Can I pet her?" he asked Nancy.

"Of course!" she replied.

Macey scooted over to Adrian, then crawled onto his lap. The boy smiled widely and petted his new friend.

"I like to hang out with dogs," Adrian said. "They're like kids to me."

When Adrian first met with Nancy, he was so shy he did not utter a single word. And then for a long while, he had difficulty putting together a coherent sentence.

It frustrated him terribly, and the communication difficulties tended to put off the other kids at his school. Adrian struggled with self-esteem and patience, and he harbored so much "chaotic energy," as his parents, Dora Jimenez and Christopher Phillips, described it, that they were terrified he might impulsively run into the street at any moment.

Even the littlest thing in everyday life could be a struggle.

"Imagine trying to go to the grocery store with a kid who can't wait in line without going into a meltdown," said Dora. "And when we'd go to museums, we had to go at the off-hours, because Adrian didn't have the patience to stand in line."

Adrian was doing much better these days, and his parents credited his time with Nancy and therapy dogs as a big reason for the improvement.

For starters, therapy dogs did not get frustrated when a kid had a hard time formulating a coherent sentence. They did not judge. They did not condescend. Their affection was natural.

Among medical professionals, animal therapy has come to be viewed as a valuable tool. Even the Mayo Clinic was now using more than a dozen registered therapy dogs and handlers. Mayo has asserted that animal assisted therapy could "reduce pain and anxiety in people with a range of health problems."

Nancy taught Adrian to play a game with Macey.

He would ask the dog a yes–no question. And the dog would respond by pawing at a button on a game.

One button would light up with "Yes" and another button prompted a "No."

It was a way to motivate a child to work on formulating sentences. And since the dog would naturally paw at the wrong button roughly half of the time, it was an example to the child that even a lovable creature like Macey could sometimes make mistakes, just like the rest of us, and not be judged.

"It teaches Adrian to try to do his best and that if you make a mistake, it's okay," said his mom. "You just need to be patient and try to follow instructions, just like the dog does."

Adrian's dad, Christopher, who wore sandals, a cabdriver cap and sunglasses tucked into the collar of his t-shirt, was thrilled to see the progress his son had made.

"It's expanded his imagination and gregariousness," said Christopher, who sat with Adrian's mom, rooting for their boy. "The affirmation is so valuable. It's been so good for Adrian's self-esteem."

The dad added: "He had been in his own little world and this has really helped bring him out."

Like many kids with special needs, Adrian also possessed special gifts. He was a whiz at math. He could make calculations in an instant that would leave others dumbfounded.

As an example, when he was told that Macey's birthday was February 15, Adrian mentioned, in a matter-of-fact way, an interesting factoid:

"February 15 was a Tuesday this year," he said. "It'll be a Wednesday next year."

This was on a Sunday in August. Most people wouldn't have a clue about a random date from six months ago.

That was nothing. Adrian could go back centuries. Give him a date in 1625, for example, and he could instantly identify if it was a Saturday or a Tuesday.

Asked how he could do this, he just shrugged. He wondered why everyone else couldn't do it.

He didn't find his talent to be very interesting. He quickly turned his attention back to Macey.

A wrinkly-faced old pup, at the relatively advanced age of fourteen, Macey could no longer hear very well. She responded mostly to hand signals.

"She'll be retiring before long," said Nancy, who was the dog's owner, as well as her partner in the therapy sessions.

With a look of concern, Adrian asked Nancy how long dogs could be expected to live.

Nancy explained that it depended on the breed and the size of the dog, but that a puggle like Macey would usually be expected to live between thirteen and fifteen years.

A look of worry flashed across Adrian's face.

"I wish," he said plaintively, "that they lived longer than thirteen to fifteen years."

His parents had seen many examples of his growing empathy since working with therapy dogs.

A few years earlier, he didn't always connect with the idea that other living beings had feelings or worth.

He once smashed a caterpillar outside their home and his mom gently chastised him, explaining that the caterpillar hadn't done anything to warrant being harmed. It was on its way to a beautiful transformation, she told him, a miracle of nature, and now that had been stopped.

His parents soon got another caterpillar and raised it to become a butterfly. Adrian made the connection.

"He was so protective," his mom said. "He understood that it's a life that needs to be cared for and loved."

She believed that his caring for therapy dogs had played a big role in his maturing sense of empathy.

Macey's next customer was Tynan, who went by the nickname T-Bone. When he was asked his age, he said that he was "twelve and two-thirds."

Tynan wore a shirt emblazoned with a photograph of himself with his pup, Cubby, named for the Chicago Cubs. (His cat, meanwhile, was named White Sox, the other Chicago baseball team.) On his shirt beneath the photograph were the words: "Tynan [heart emoji] Dogs."

The first thing someone might notice about Tynan was his withered right arm and the large red birthmark that covered half of his face.

These features were the consequence of a congenital brain disease called Sturge-Weber syndrome, a vascular disorder that had triggered constant seizures.

When he was four, he had a serious surgery to address the seizures. Surgeons performed a radical procedure known as a hemispherectomy, removing the diseased half of Tynan's brain.

As he played with Macey, Tynan talked about the innate goodness and dependability of dogs.

"When your dad is at work and your mom is busy and your grandpa is asleep," Tynan explained, "you can always play with a dog."

The first time Nancy Endow heard about therapy dogs, many years earlier, she didn't have a clue about them, and she readily acknowledged she was more than a bit skeptical.

Is this really going to help? she wondered.

When her son was twenty, he had brought home a puggle he named Mason, a dog that was hit and killed by a car several months later. The week after the dog died, Nancy's family brought home another puggle and named her Macey.

"She became the love of our life," said Nancy.

During a training session with Macey, a trainer suggested that she might make a good therapy dog. She encouraged Nancy to think about it and attend a therapy session.

"The more I saw and learned, the more intrigued I became," said Nancy, who had recently turned sixty-eight. "And I thought this is something I could do in my retirement."

Therapy dogs and their handlers worked together as a team, so Nancy and Macey were trained together. When Nancy started volunteering, she quickly saw the bonds between dogs and kids. She found herself moved, and signed up to volunteer with Macey.

Working with kids and adults with special needs, she saw them overcome feelings of deep isolation, anxiety, even a sense of inferiority. She was amazed at how quickly the therapy could make a difference.

While working with the over-eighteen group, participants were asked before the therapy sessions how they rated their feelings, on a one to ten scale. Afterwards, they were asked the same question.

Almost without fail, the numbers went up after the dog therapy. With children, she said, the results were even more striking.

"It gave them a focus other than their disability or disease," said Nancy.

She was so touched that she took in another dog, Layla, and trained with her for therapy, too.

For the handler, the therapy required a lot of work and creativity. It was a serious commitment and took up many Sundays. She has never been paid a dime, of course, but she considered herself well-compensated.

"It's the thrill you see in the eyes of the kids," she said. "That's what really counts for me."

CHAPTER FOURTEEN

SISTERHOOD

In the lobby of the Iowa City Public Library, seven-year-old Caroline hid under a bench, then scooched as far back against the wall as she could, so that nobody could see her.

Her "big sister," Alisa Pursley, a college student, bent to her knees and used a gentle voice to try to convince the little girl to come out of hiding and meet someone who wanted to say hello.

Despite Alisa's pleadings, Caroline, who was very shy, remained under the bench for what seemed a very long time.

She was not anxious to meet anyone.

Alisa remained patient and, at long last, the adorable little Caroline, with her long, dark ponytail and multicolored sneakers, rolled out from under the bench and rose to her feet. She immediately reached up for Alisa's hand, a source of comfort, and they walked together, ready to face the world.

For the past eighteen months, Alisa and Caroline had bonded in the Big Brothers Big Sisters program. Alisa's outstretched hand offered stability in a life that had sometimes been rocky.

Until recently, Caroline hadn't seen her mom in more than a year. These days, she was spending the weekdays with a grandmother, and alternating weekends between her father and mother in two different towns.

That was a lot of shuttling around. And when she was in one place, of course, she wasn't in the other.

"It makes me sad," said Caroline.

Caroline's father—Da, as she calls him—had asked if she might like to have a big sister. Caroline thought that sounded nice. So they went to the Iowa City office of the Big Brothers Big Sisters and had a talk with a nice lady there.

Around the same time, Alisa had been watching the *Today* show and saw a segment on the Big Brothers Big Sisters program and thought, "That's something I could do."

She filled out an application, provided letters of reference, and submitted to a background check.

Soon afterward, the phone rang, and a woman at Big Brothers Big Sisters delivered the good news.

"I think we have a match for you," the woman told Alisa. "Her name is Caroline."

When they first met, Caroline was very timid with Alisa. But before long, the two of them would be hanging out talking and going fishing, whizzing around the playground, and bouncing at the trampoline park. The goal was to spend six hours together every month.

"She's nice," Caroline said of Alisa, breaking into a smile and nodding her head. "I like having someone to play with."

On this Friday afternoon, they had big plans. After the visit to the library, they were going to the playground—Caroline was in a mighty hurry to get there—and then they were going to the Pizza Ranch to get something to eat and play arcade games.

Alisa, a junior at the University of Iowa in her hometown of Iowa City, had long been a champion volunteer. For her Vacation Bible School, she raked lawns and paid visits to the elderly. As she grew older, she took on a bigger challenge. She was the director of a dance marathon that served as a fundraiser for a children's hospital. In the span of four years, the event had raised some $30,000.

When she met Caroline, she was eager to find out what the little girl liked. A girl of few words, at least until she trusts someone, Caroline told Alisa that she was a big fan of *Pokémon*, and that her favorite color was green.

Alisa promptly began doing research on *Pokémon*. She also made it a point to stay current with Disney movies so that she could be fluent in the language of young people.

These days, Caroline's favorite game was *Among Us*, an online space-themed adventure. At the library, she found a dry-erase board and began drawing some characters from the game. She chose to draw the figures using the green-colored marker, naturally.

Every time she met up with Caroline, Alisa recited these words: "You're brave, you're beautiful, and you're strong."

"No," Caroline responded the first time, shaking her head.

"Yes!" said Alisa.

Before long, Caroline was reciting—with conviction—that she was, indeed, brave, beautiful and strong.

"We're building confidence and working on the positive," Alisa explained. "I try to promote the idea that she can do whatever she wants when she grows up. We're working on building expectations. The more she hears those things out loud, the more she will believe it."

"What are you good at?" Alisa asked Caroline.

"Math," Caroline replied.

"And soccer," Alisa reminded her.

"I play on a team," Caroline said, with a nod. "And I get to run a lot."

Before Alisa met Caroline, she was majoring in art therapy. Her experience with Caroline prompted her to switch her major to elementary education.

"I learn just as much from Caroline as she learns from me—how to play, let go, have patience," she said. "I saw how much progress we could make in a short amount of time."

Alisa would soon be doing her student teaching in Houston, Texas, which would be exciting, but it was "pretty likely" she would return to Iowa City when it's time to settle down.

For her part, Caroline said she planned to be a doctor.

"I like to help people," she explained.

She had the right impulses, Alisa said. When they arrived at the library, Caroline, before seeking refuge under the bench, held the door for people coming behind her.

And where exactly would seven-year-old Caroline like to live when she grows up and becomes a doctor?

She didn't miss a beat.

"With my mom."

CHAPTER FIFTEEN

FROM A BOULDER TO A STONE

At the funeral inside St. Anne's Catholic Church in Barrington, Illinois, a man she did not know handed a pamphlet to Mary Ann O'Rourke, a mother so crushed by grief and guilt she could scarcely speak.

When Mary Ann and her husband, Leo Burns, went home after the services, she left the pamphlet on a countertop where it stayed untouched for days, then weeks, then months since that tragic day when their son, Joe, was found in a crawl space in the basement. He had hanged himself with a tae kwon do belt. He had just turned twenty.

The coroner found a note in the pocket of his jeans. The final handwritten words from young Joseph Fisher Burns read:

> *I'm sorry. It's nobody's fault. I'm just not cut out for it.*
> *Peace and love, Joe.*

The younger of two boys, Joe had been a happy-go-lucky kid growing up, doing backflips into the swimming pool and executing breathtaking Black Diamond glides down the ski slopes.

"He was a daredevil," said his mother. "He had no fear."

He was very popular with friends. On his birthdays, his parents would throw a "tent-out party" in the backyard, with friends spending the night in each of three or four pop-up tents. The other boys would fight with one another over who got to stay in the tent with Joe.

Joe grew up playing sports. His dad coached him in youth baseball and football. The kid loved fishing. He was a big fan of the Chicago Bears. He could recite all kinds of arcane sports statistics and rattle off the Super Bowl winners for every year. He was thoughtful and creative and had a talent for writing.

But Joe struggled with academics. Teachers said he would sit in class and stare into space, seemingly deep in thought about something. He was diagnosed with attention deficit disorder.

After graduating from Barrington High School, he went to Southern Illinois University. He did not do well in his classes. At the end of his first school year, he moved home to attend nearby Harper College and worked part-time as a dishwasher.

Barrington, among the most affluent of Chicago suburbs, cultivated a majestic aura with its brick mansions, lavish country clubs, and rolling horse pastures. But not everyone in the town was rich.

Mary Ann and Leo did well enough financially. She had worked in public relations at Hill & Knowlton, and then at the Sears headquarters in corporate communication until she was laid off. Leo worked at the Chicago Board of Trade, a commodity exchange. They were a middle-class family and lived in a modest ranch home.

"We never had a lot of money," said Mary Ann. "But there's a lot of wealth out here. And I worry sometimes that Joe didn't feel like he was up to snuff in this crowd."

She was concerned, moreover, that his difficulties in school only exacerbated those self-esteem issues.

"His friends were all going to Big Ten schools and they would come home and brag about their college experiences," she said. "And Joe was listening to all of this and he was failing at SIU."

And then a series of missteps—the kind of mistakes common in teenage life—seem to have left Joe feeling that he was at the end of the road.

At a party across the street from his home, he was cited for underage drinking. Under the state's zero tolerance law, that meant a loss of driving privileges.

Weeks later, when his license arrived in the mail—apparently sent by someone who found it—Joe believed that his suspension had ended and that he was now legally allowed to drive.

He was mistaken.

When an acquaintance called late one night, saying he was in a bad spot and needed a ride home, Joe, believing he could legally drive, charged out into the night to rescue the young man.

On the ride back, police lights flashed in the rearview mirror and Joe was pulled over. The cop ran a check on his driver's license. It was invalid. Driving on a suspended license was a serious offense.

To make matters worse, his young passenger had a can of beer. Joe had not had anything to drink. But as the driver, he was charged under the law forbidding any open container of alcohol in a vehicle.

He did not tell his parents about the trouble. He holed up in his bedroom.

"Joe's in bad trouble," his older brother, Jack, told their mother, explaining what had happened.

Mary Ann marched into the bedroom, where Joe was hiding under a blanket. She reprimanded him. It was the kind of reaction any parent could understand in a moment of exasperation. But it would later haunt her.

On Joe's court date, he was nowhere to be found. As the hours passed and night fell, his worried parents finally called the police.

A squad car arrived at the home and officers conducted a search, but did not find him. A while later, one of Mary Ann's sisters came to the house and asked if she could check the basement, almost as if she had a premonition.

Mary Ann followed her down the stairs. When her sister looked in the crawl space, she let out a horrified scream. Mary Ann shouted desperately for Leo, then collapsed on the floor.

When Leo came down and saw his son, he fell to his knees and lay down beside him.

In shock, Mary Ann could not talk. In the aftermath, she did not remember everything about that horrifying night. But she did remember a crippling pain in her stomach. She remembered dry heaving over the toilet.

Her sister called a doctor, who prescribed a powerful sedative for Mary Ann. Someone picked it up from the pharmacy. Gradually, she was able to utter some words.

Jack, who was then twenty-two, had been out looking for his younger brother when his cell phone rang.

It was a cousin calling.

"We found Joe... he's gone."

Jack, horrified, angry and helpless, walked through the door at home and started throwing furniture around in a fit of rage.

Leo, a native of Kansas City, and one of eleven siblings, called his family to tell them his son had taken his life.

When the news reached his brothers and sisters—wherever each of them happened to be at the moment—they got into their cars and pointed toward Illinois.

Every one of them.

A priest from St. Anne's arrived at the house and gathered with the family on the back porch.

"I'm not a very religious person," said Mary Ann, who wore a sleeve on her arm for a condition related to breast cancer treatments. "But it was soothing to hear his words."

The guilt lay heavy, though, especially as she replayed in her mind the scolding she had given to Joe for getting into trouble with the law.

"He's a sensitive kid. If only I'd said this. If only I'd said that."

A handful of years later, she sat and gazed at a photograph of Joe, a handsome young man, leaning his head affectionately against his mother's shoulder. The picture was taken just months before he took his life.

The pamphlet that Mary Ann had received at the funeral, the one that lay for so long on the countertop, came from a member of a group called LOSS (Loving Outreach to Survivors of Suicide). The man who had given the pamphlet to her had also lost a son to suicide.

The group met one Wednesday a month at seven o'clock in the evening in the basement of Holy Family Parish in the nearby suburb of Inverness.

Six months after Joe's death, Mary Ann and Leo, with no small measure of trepidation, walked through the doors to attend a session with the group of other bereaved family members.

They had to try something.

"I had spent the last six months crying," Mary Ann said.

Leo, meanwhile, had been stoic, emotionally bottled up, focused on staying in control. But when it came time for him to speak at the meeting, he sobbed so relentlessly he could barely get words out of his mouth. People nearby leaned over and rubbed his back.

"I thought, 'Thank God,'" said Mary Ann. "That's what he needed."

Mary Ann heard some things she needed to hear, too. The group helped mightily with guilt and anger.

"We learned that this wasn't about us," said Mary Ann. "Joe was suffering something terrible. He was trying to end his suffering. That's what this was about."

The leaders of the group promised a better day would come.

"I remember someone saying, 'This grief is like a rock. First it's like carrying a boulder. It's so big and heavy that you can't stand or walk. Over time, it will become a very big rock, and you can move slowly. Eventually, it becomes a stone. It will always be with you. But you can put it in your pocket.'"

Mary Ann remembered, "I couldn't wait for that stone."

Like many other support groups, each person in LOSS was essentially a volunteer for the others. As the months, and then years passed, Mary Ann became regarded as one of the senior people in the group, and was asked to serve as the moderator.

In any way she could, she reached out to those who might need support after losing a loved one to suicide. She used social media to call out to those who were suffering.

Our son would have celebrated his twenty-fifth birthday today, she posted on Facebook on June 28, 2021, displaying more than a dozen photographs of Joe.

I love these photos because they help me focus on the beautiful twenty years we had with him, she wrote. *I can't imagine getting through these past five years without LOSS.*

Certainly, a club no one wants to join—but sharing this grief with others who have had this experience—has helped us tremendously.

Love you forever, Joe.

After Joe was cremated, the urn was taken to a cemetery in Kansas City, to be with Burns family members. A small portion of the ashes were placed in a heart-shaped locket that Mary Ann wore around her neck.

At the LOSS meetings, Mary Ann paid careful attention to the newcomers. They were so beaten, so raw. She knew that feeling in her bones.

Now as the volunteer serving as a leader for the group, she was able to tell them:

"When this first happens, some people say, 'Time heals all wounds,' and you just want to punch them in the face."

She went on:

"But the sun will shine again. And someday you'll laugh and you'll feel guilty for laughing. Life does go on. Sometimes you'll need to pull off the road and sob. Then you get back on the road and you move forward.

"This is a process. You might not feel like it now, but you are moving forward."

CHAPTER SIXTEEN

THE KID MADE A MISTAKE

The offender stood in the middle of the hearing room, facing eight jurors sitting along a long white table, an American flag behind them, in a police department northwest of Chicago.

On this icy night in November, the offender would give his version of what he had done wrong, why he had gone astray, and whether there was anything troubling going on in his life.

He might have been apprehended for shoplifting, illegal possession of drugs, battery, vandalism.

The jurors would pepper him with questions.

"Why did you do it?" a juror, Matt Czyzewski, has asked some of the offenders outright.

"What were you thinking about?"

"How did your parents and coaches feel about this?"

"How has it affected the community?"

The offender and the jurors were all under age eighteen. This peer jury, which convened twice a month, was composed of volunteers from Prospect High School.

The police had given the offenders a choice to go to court, where a guilty verdict would result in a fine, and possibly other punishment, or go through the peer jury system, which did not impose fines or legal consequences.

"It's meant to be restorative, not punitive," said Detective Lisa Schaps, who oversaw the program. "It's diversionary. We want to keep them out of the system. They're not cuffed or fingerprinted. It's all about changing behavior."

The jurors would not determine the guilt or innocence of the fellow teenager. Instead, they would hear out the offender, then dismiss him from the room for a time so they could talk among themselves, along with a trained counselor, about the "sentence" to impose.

Detective Schaps would read the police reports to the jurors, so they could compare the official account to the description given by the offenders, as a way to assess how honest and forthcoming each of them had been.

The sentence decreed by the jury would range from two to twenty hours of community service, and perhaps an assignment to write a letter to the people who were harmed by the unlawful actions.

To help them make restitution, the offenders were given a list of local nonprofit organizations that needed help with staffing, such as food pantries, social service volunteer groups, or charities.

The offenders were given one month to complete the duties assigned by the jurors, and then were required to return to show proof of the community service, and to share with the jurors what they had learned from the experience.

If an offender did not return for the second hearing, or failed to complete the assigned duties, the case would be referred to the court for adjudication.

Some of the offenders appeared before the peer jury with an obvious feeling of embarrassment and remorse. Others displayed a hard pose—what the volunteer juror, Matt, described as "a lot of attitude."

"They might look at the floor, cross their arms, and kind of grunt one-word answers to questions," said Matt. "One kid even said he only agreed to come because it was a 'get-out-of-jail-free card.'"

Those chip-on-the-shoulder episodes, however, were in the minority. In most cases, the offenders came across as sincere, honest, and filled with regret. It was not uncommon for offenders to shed tears as they talked about their misdeeds.

Even some of those offenders who acted so tough during the first round, said Matt, would return with a humble demeanor, having learned from the process how their actions had caused problems for others.

"Going to court is scary, but fear doesn't usually work," said Matt. "And for people who come from families with money, they just have their parents pay the fine and that's the end of it. But in this process, they have to really think about what they did."

When he was younger, Matt was interested in a career in law enforcement. As a high school sophomore, he had asked a police officer if he could go on a "ride-along" in the squad car. The officer told him he was too young, but pointed him to the peer jury program.

"I gave it a try and I fell in love with it," he said, explaining that "a minor can connect with another minor on a level" that an adult might not be able to reach.

In a view that might seem paradoxical, Matt said his three years on the jury had actually made him more sensitive to the challenges facing young people who had gotten themselves into trouble.

"I always had this mindset, 'Why would you do something like that?'" he said. "But when you listen to them, you might find out that there's been a romantic breakup, or somebody in the family has just died, maybe their parents have recently gotten divorced. It could be that they suffer from depression or anxiety. It's not that they're bad or dumb. People sometimes fall.

"We're there to try to pick them up."

Some of the offenders have gone through the process and become peer jury volunteers themselves.

Another juror, Gabriella Swanson, wore a puffy green hooded sweatshirt, emblazoned with USMC, for the Marine Corps. At sixteen, she hoped to become a police officer someday.

She said she was motivated to look out for others because she had endured severe bullying herself, much of it online.

"Somebody posted that I should kill myself," she said.

It was a taunt so cruel it would be hard to imagine being aimed at anyone, much less a kid like Gabriella, who exuded kindness.

She had been targeted, she said, "because I don't dress like other girls—I don't conform."

When her mother learned about the bullying, Gabriella said, she called the school and demanded that it stop.

"She protected me," said Gabriella, saying her mother's actions seemed to reflect the values of a cop. "I decided that I wanted to protect people, too."

She said the peer jury was like a family. In the view of plenty of kids at school, however, it was uncool.

"They think we're traitors," she said. "They think we're like the police and they think the police are awful."

It was an odd take, given that the peer jury sought to give kids in trouble a chance to avoid the legal system.

Not everyone at school saw it negatively, including some who had gone through it as offenders.

A girl that Gabriella's jury had sentenced was in her psychology class. Neither said a word about their shared history, though both certainly remembered.

"She was really nice," said Gabriella. "She just made a mistake."

Luis Hernandez, a seventeen-year-old volunteer juror, was born in the United States, moved to Mexico when he was one, and returned at age twelve. He intended to major in theater when he went to college.

Maybe it was the drama of the legal system that piqued his interest and prompted him to join the peer jury.

"I always liked those cop shows," he said, with a chuckle.

But the first time he came to the peer jury, he confessed, he felt very uncomfortable.

"It was scary," he said. "It was in a police station. In Mexico, the police station was not a place you wanted to be."

The anxieties melted when he met others in the jury and saw for himself the positive changes the program could forge.

Kids who were acting out, he noticed, were often going through difficult family problems at home.

"Some of them don't even *have* parents, just a guardian," Luis said. "When I heard a kid talk about how his parents weren't in the picture, I just wanted to go give him a hug."

CHAPTER SEVENTEEN

FEELING COOL AT LAST

Going through school, Sarah Cornett often found herself feeling awfully lonely.

"I have a disability that affects my social skills," explained Sarah, who was diagnosed with autism at age two. "I'm uncomfortable around people."

A teacher in her school recommended that she consider joining a club called Cool Aspies, a social group for those living on the autism spectrum.

"It's awesome—I love it," said Sarah, who was twenty-two. "I have made friends."

The group, based in Alexandria, Virginia, met once a month to share in a group activity: laser tag, yoga, riverboat excursions, museum trips, water parks, a comedy class.

Another club member, Alejandro Ifarragu, talked excitedly about the group going rope climbing and sitting in the stands at a Washington Nationals baseball game.

"It's nice to do things I've never done before," he said.

For Thomas Davis, who belonged to the club for a decade and now served as a mentor to the younger people, Cool Aspies had been a life-changer.

Once feeling "sort of by myself," he said, he could now count on more than eight friends. And one of them was very special.

"It's how I met Ariel, my girlfriend," he said. "We consider ourselves best friends. We go to movies and dinners. And she's a great artist."

With shared challenges, Ariel and Thomas are there for each other.

Thomas had a fear of heights. When he sensed that he was up too high, like when he was standing on a balcony, he would feel panic coming on. He would reach for Ariel's grasp.

"She holds my hand and squeezes it," he said, "and that makes the fear go away."

The founder and leader of the club was Deborah Hammer, a volunteer for a national group, the Organization for Autism Research (OAR).

A teacher in her early fifties, Deborah could relate to the members of the club. She, too, was living with autism.

The club grew out of a meeting Deborah had one summer afternoon with some former students on the autism spectrum. They had expressed frustrations with a lack of social connections and a sense of belonging.

"They chose the name Cool Aspies," said Deborah, who described her role as the club's facilitator. "Growing up with autism, people are often not given the opportunity to make choices. Things are decided for you."

Deborah helped the club members build the confidence to become more assertive and advocate for themselves, as well as recognize boundaries.

In her case, Deborah's parents sensed that "I was different, a little quirky" when she was about three years old.

"I would go into my own world," she said. "And I would wave my hands a lot."

Because she was an early reader and communicated effectively, however, she was initially not diagnosed with autism.

The diagnosis would come many years later, when she was a student at the University of Georgia. Pursuing a degree in special education, she read about the characteristics of autism and realized that "I could see myself."

When a doctor told Deborah that she was, indeed, autistic, it was a catharsis, a confirmation of her belief that her brain worked differently.

For a long time, she kept the diagnosis to herself.

"I was afraid of the stigma," she said. "I worried, 'Will I be able to get hired?'"

Even her family discouraged her from telling people about her autism.

The autism spectrum is a wide range, Deborah noted, from people who could not talk or tie their shoes to those who were excelling in graduate school.

In earlier days, Deborah was described as "high-functioning," but that term was now discouraged. It implied a sort of hierarchy. Instead, a person like her is simply described as having fewer support needs.

What had been called Asperger syndrome, once considered a milder condition—and therefore a diagnosis seen as favorable by many parents of kids with autism—has given way in professional circles to simply being recognized as a place on the autism spectrum.

While the characteristics varied, autism was often marked by a difficulty with social skills and the tendency to exhibit a fascination with a particular subject and focus on it intensely.

In Deborah's case, it was bats. It still is.

Beloved in her school district, Deborah was busy almost every night and on weekends, serving in some way to "give back," from being a leader in her homeowners association to participating in a bat welfare group.

As a key volunteer for OAR, she was part of a team helping to advance the use of science in addressing the social, educational and treatment concerns of those on the spectrum. The association also promoted better understanding of autism among the parents and teachers in their lives.

OAR has cited studies that found that kids and young adults on the autism spectrum frequently faced severe isolation, even when compared to others with disabilities.

"Young adults with autism," one study found, "were significantly more likely to never see friends or be invited to activities, compared to those with intellectual disabilities, learning disabilities, or emotional disabilities."

The group had raised more than $4 million since 2002 for autism research in the form of pilot studies, and more than $300,000 in graduate research grants. OAR had also awarded more than $1 million in scholarships to nearly 400 people with autism attending college or vocational technical schools.

The organization produced a guide for best practices in education, as well as producing a "Hire Autism" portal that connected adults on the spectrum with prospective employees.

Among her many contributions to OAR, Deborah wrote a blog, as well as published an article titled, "How to Start a Self-Determination Club at Your School."

In many schools, she noted, those with a disability have what was known as an Individualized Education Plan (IEP) that plotted a course for success best-suited to the needs of a particular student.

For the most part, these plans were put together with input from parents, teachers and therapists.

"But the student was excluded," said Deborah.

These were young people who already feel left out of too many facets of their lives. That would not be the case when Deborah was around. She made sure that the young people with autism she encountered got a positive message about themselves. She was a perfect role model.

"I'm not ashamed of it," said Deborah, noting that people with autism often have an extraordinary ability to focus on things that matter to them.

"I view it as my superpower," she said.

CHAPTER EIGHTEEN

IN THE NAME OF HIS FATHER

As a teenager nearly a century ago in the factory town of Kenosha, Wisconsin, young Justin "Judd" Goldman was making quite a mark as an athlete, especially on the basketball court and the baseball diamond.

This kid, everyone said, had real talent.

A bone disease, however, would curtail the sports career for Judd. For a lauded young athlete, it was a difficult blow. As a result of the illness, one leg was two inches shorter than the other. He needed to be fitted with special shoes.

With the guidance of an uncle who owned a boat, Judd ventured out on the waters of Lake Michigan along the Wisconsin shoreline, learning how to navigate. Over the years, he would become an accomplished sailor.

Judd went on to marry, become the father of two children, and start a successful paint manufacturing business.

At age seventy-five, a month before his unexpected death in 1989, Judd had a talk with his son, Peter, about the emotional and psychological importance of his experiences in a sailboat as someone with a physical disability.

"He said if it wasn't for sailing, it would have been very tough for him," recalled Peter, his voice heavy with emotion all these years later, reflecting on his father's struggles. "I was forty-five at the time, and this was a conversation we had never had."

Peter, who learned to sail at camp, had himself become a star on the waters, talented enough to compete at the trials for the U.S. Olympic Games of 1964, though he did not make the team.

He went on to become a successful entrepreneur, a maker of automobile polish in Chicago.

His father's words about the importance of sailing for a disabled person had moved and inspired him. Just a month after his dad's death, he turned to his mother, Sliv, and raised the idea of starting a sailing program for the disabled.

She was all for it.

"There's a lot more to life than car polish," she told him.

With three boats and the help of friends and family members, the program was launched. In the early years, Peter's mother did the cooking for the volunteers and the participants.

Over three decades, the Judd Goldman Adaptive Sailing Foundation would grow to a charity that taught and sponsored more than 10,000 disabled people in the sport of sailing. Some 98 percent of them had never before been on a sailboat.

The program provided classroom and on-the-water instruction. The fleet grew to consist of some twenty sailboats and several motorboats. All boats had been adapted to fit the needs of the disabled and engineered so they would not capsize. The special equipment included transfer boarding benches that assisted sailors moving from wheelchairs to seats. The student to instructor ratio, meanwhile, was one-to-two.

The capstone of the sailing season was the Independence Cup, a series of races in Burnham Harbor at the shore of Lake Michigan in Chicago. It was billed as the premier regatta for physically disabled sailors.

On a breezy weekend in July, sunlight glimmered off the stainless steel of a flurry of wheelchairs. Some of these racers were blind. Others were struggling with cancer. Still others had been severely disabled in an accident. One struggled with the aftermath of childhood polio.

Each racing team included three participants, including one able-bodied person. Among the sailors, the sense of triumph and accomplishment seemed to soar like the nearby dazzling skyscrapers that stood for Chicago's might and ambition.

Young Kim, a fifty-nine-year-old survivor of childhood polio, raced on a boat named *Impossible Dream*. In his wheelchair, he gathered with teammates afterwards at a picnic table to celebrate. It was his first sailboat race in his life.

"Third place—not bad!" he said, sitting in his wheelchair, smiling broadly and sipping an Anti-Hero beer. "I can now call myself a bona fide sailor."

A retired information technology professional, Young was born in Korea and diagnosed with polio when he was three months old. His family would move to the United States when he was eleven.

As a child in Korea, he remembered, he was teased about his condition. He said people with disabilities were expected to stay out of view, a stigma that left him severely isolated.

"I didn't have much exposure to the outside world," he said, "except from the stoop of my house."

He depended on crutches until he was thirty, when he began using a wheelchair. Pain was a constant in his life. But while racing in the vast blue waters of Lake Michigan, he said, something seemingly magical would happen.

"I forget my pain."

Another sailor, Bridgette, who was forty-five, had lost a leg in a motorcycle accident nearly twenty years earlier. She learned about the sailing program when she met Peter Goldman in the lobby of a rehabilitation institute at Northwestern Memorial Hospital.

"I was so depressed," said Bridgette, who lived with her fourteen-year-old son, Sebu, in a 450-square-foot apartment in Chicago. There was no room for a bedroom for her. She slept in the dining room. Her son's father had left when she was nine months pregnant.

Peter could sense that she was in a dark place.

"Hey, you ever try sailing?" he asked her.

She decided to give it a try. She took some lessons and soon became a racer.

"Sailing opened me up to realize I could do stuff," said Bridgette. "Being on the water is energetic. You have to pay attention. You're constantly making adjustments. There's a lot of science, a lot of math, and a lot of spirituality. It reminds me that I am equal to everyone else, rich or homeless. We're all joined together by nature."

Everyone in the adaptive sailing circuit had a story, she said, and the sense of community served as a buoy. She only wished that more disabled people would join them.

"There are people sitting in their homes, just hoping someone comes to visit," she said. "They should be out here sailing."

For all of her challenges, she said, she had come to focus on the bright parts of her life and future. Her son was an honors student at the highly regarded Lincoln Park High School. And she was pursuing career aspirations that once seemed impossible.

A striking woman with an outgoing personality, Bridgette had recently learned about a growing acknowledgment in the entertainment business that disabled people, at long last, should be cast in acting roles.

So she auditioned for a part in a television show.

"I didn't get the part," she said. "But I got an agent!"

Peter Goldman sold his car polish company in 2018 to Energizer Battery. At seventy-seven, he said friends and acquaintances routinely described him as being retired.

He cheerfully scoffed at the notion.

"People say I'm retired, but I'm working every day," he said. "I probably would have been more successful in business if I hadn't been putting so much time into the charity."

But as his mother, Sliv, who died in 2004, told him long ago: "There's a lot more to life than car polish."

He would not argue. The sailing program had recently started an outreach to young people in struggling neighborhoods, places where few people ever have the opportunity to spend a weekend on a sailboat.

It has meant a lot to Peter Goldman to watch the joy of people celebrating their freedom after feeling captive.

More than once, he has heard testimony from participants that moved him to tears.

"Someone will say, 'If it wasn't for sailing, I might have taken my life. I was so depressed.'"

For many of the sailors who came to the race in wheelchairs, it seemed that sailing was a metaphor for life.

"When you have a disability that's thrust upon you," as one sailor said, "you adjust your sails and keep going."

CHAPTER NINETEEN

THE GIFT OF A SMILE

If people have the money, they can often buy what looks like a million-dollar smile.

People without money, in contrast, often try not to smile or talk very much in public.

They are ashamed of the condition of their teeth, said Dr. Paul Engen, a dentist retired from private practice and now working as a volunteer in the treatment of low-income people.

Without the resources to spend on oral health and repairs, they might have gone without dental care for many years, or in plenty of cases, for all of their lives.

Broken or unsightly teeth could make it more difficult to get a job, to find a partner, to be respected, and to be taken seriously in everyday encounters.

It could take a terrible toll on self-esteem.

"When you have confidence in your smile," said Dr. Engen, a bespectacled, white-haired, sixty-six-year-old, wearing scrubs and gym shoes, "it changes your personality."

For many people, the cost of such confidence was out of reach. Most private insurance plans provided relatively limited dental coverage, especially if a procedure was deemed to be cosmetic.

Medicaid, for the poor, meanwhile, provided such low reimbursement rates and required such onerous paperwork that many dental offices declined to participate in the program. Medicare, for the elderly, provided no coverage for dental services, except with a supplemental plan, and poor people were not likely able to afford the coverage.

As a result, many people were getting along with terrible dental function and poor oral hygiene, which could be a threat to more serious health conditions, including heart problems.

To help people who could not afford dental care, Dr. Engen, a soft-spoken man who stood six feet six, drove twice a month from his home in Elgin, Illinois, to a clinic in suburban Wheaton to donate his services.

To people who had long lived in shame about the condition of their teeth, the work of the kindly dentist seemed like a miracle.

After finally getting treatment and looking into the mirror, many of these patients were moved to tears. They often reached out to hug him in appreciation for changing their lives. And they smiled more broadly than they had ever smiled before.

Dr. Engen was one of the hundreds of dentists and hygienists who volunteered their services at the clinic, which was sponsored by the Chicago Dental Society.

In the past year, the clinic had served nearly four hundred patients in the course of more than one thousand appointments. About half of the dental volunteers were retired; the other half were donating time that could have been spent in private practice earning them more money.

Some of the patients arrived at the clinic in a van sent by the Pacific Garden Mission, one of the largest homeless shelters in Chicago. Others were physically abused women who had been referred by domestic violence centers. All of those who came to the clinic had little or no income.

On this rainy fall day, one woman stopped at the desk of the office manager, Geraldine Munoz, and offered her appreciation.

"Thank you for all you did to help me," she said, visibly moved.

"You're welcome," Geraldine responded warmly. "We're here to help."

Another patient was a forty-six-year-old man who had been disabled by a stroke. The man, who asked to remain anonymous, "for reasons of pride," said he did not know what he would do without the free treatment from the dentist.

"Without good teeth, how would I eat?" he asked.

An immigrant from Egypt, the man's wife was waiting in the car to pick him up. She worked as a cashier at a department store. They were the parents of two children in school, and they stretched every dollar to make ends meet.

He spent a lot of time thinking about college and the costs ahead.

"My kids get very good grades," he said proudly. "I hear about scholarships from the government, so I am hoping they can get help."

Using a cane, he moved haltingly toward the door, as the office manager called out, "You take care!"

Watching as so many people struggled, Dr. Engen knew that he had reason to be grateful. His own life had been blessed, he said, with a loving wife and four healthy and thriving children. He always felt he owed it to help others. Volunteering was among the important things he wanted to do in retirement, along with spending some precious time with his wife.

"She has some health issues," he said. "We need to take advantage of the time we have."

Doing good works seemed to have run in Dr. Engen's family. His father was a pastor and his mother was a nurse.

His cousin, Kari Engen, meanwhile, had moved to Guatemala as a teenager to work with the poor. She was still there more than thirty years later.

She lived and worked in the Guatemala City Dump. It has been described as the poorest and most violent place in the country. Families scavenged for discarded food to eat and salvaged sheets of cardboard to build little shacks, even as vultures circled overhead.

Kari opened a school for the children living in the dump—Mi Refugio, which translated to *my refuge*—providing education, food, clothing and medical treatment.

Her work became the subject of a documentary, *Children of the Fourth World*, as well as television reports that inspired viewers to donate goods to Guatemalans in desperate need.

When two American surgeons saw a segment about a little boy who was missing an arm, they flew to Guatemala to examine the child and arranged for a prosthesis to be designed for him.

Dr. Engen was inspired to follow his cousin to Guatemala and help the poor children there, too.

"They had no dental care, so I went there and started a clinic."

What he would see in Guatemala moved him deeply. Over the years, he would make eight visits to the school in the dump—ten days at a time—to help as many Guatemalans as possible.

"These were people living in shacks, dirt floors, no running water, struggling every day to find food," he said. "I'm not a person that shows a lot of emotion, but it affected me deeply."

His wife spoke Spanish and worked as a translator. Dr. Engen treated young children who had never received dental care, and whose "every baby tooth was rotted to the gumline."

He saw patients in such excruciating pain they had difficulty eating.

He became familiar with a world where children were sexually exploited, severely beaten, even murdered.

In the suburbs of the American Midwest where he worked, such widespread and desperate poverty might seem hard to imagine. But even in the comparative land of plenty, he had seen countless cases of economic despair.

As he knew, people were counting on his volunteerism, and he vowed to carry on "as long as my health and my back hold up—and I think that's going to be awhile."

CHAPTER TWENTY

A GUY NAMED SCOTT BAUER

Jeff and Diane Shultz, along with their ten-year-old son, Max, and eight-year-old daughter, Hannah, were very excited about taking a spontaneous trip to Traverse City, Michigan, a family getaway in August before the start of a new school year.

On the first day of the trek, they drove as far as Holland, Michigan, where they relaxed at the beach, went out for a delicious dinner, and then watched a gorgeous sunset.

Jeff, who had been working intensely on a sales deal, was able to unwind. He seemed delightfully carefree.

"It was the most perfect day," said Diane.

They checked into a large room at the Doubletree Hilton, and made plans for the next day. An hour or so after the kids went to sleep, Jeff and Diane cozied up and closed their eyes.

When Jeff suddenly made a strange noise, Diane reached over and whispered *shush*, afraid he would wake the children. When he kept making the sound, she tugged at his arm and then rose up and looked at him. His eyes were closed and she was unable to rouse him.

Frantic, she dialed the front desk and told them to call 911 immediately.

"I was freaking out," said Diane.

Jeff began shaking and sweating profusely. Before the ambulance arrived, a hotel worker rushed to the room and began to perform CPR. Another employee, meanwhile, woke the kids and took them to another room, where they watched TV and finally fell asleep.

The paramedics arrived and carried Jeff to an ambulance. One of the medics soon returned to the room.

"I'm sorry," he told Diane. "He didn't make it."

Jeff was forty-five.

Diane went into shock, gasping and trembling, and collapsed on the bed, screaming into the mattress.

"This can't be happening! It's a terrible dream!"

She reached for her phone and called her husband's best friend and wife to tell them the terrible news.

"We're coming to get you," they told her.

The friends arrived at four or five in the morning to embrace Diane, all three of them crying. When the kids were awakened, they saw their distraught mother and instantly asked, "How's Papa?"

Diane could barely get the words out.

"He's not going to be able to come home with us," she told them. "The ambulance came and tried to help him. But he didn't make it."

As their friends drove them back to Chicago in a hard rain, Diane and the kids sobbed for hours.

Even now, years later, Diane could not clearly remember the events of the few days that followed her husband's death from cardiac arrest. She recalled that people were giving her lists of things to do: call the funeral home, inform the employer, check on insurance.

A friend, who also had lost her young husband a couple of years earlier, told her:

"You need to talk to a guy named Scott Bauer."

Not long afterward, Diane's phone rang. It was Scott.

"He said, 'I'm here for you. I'm here for your kids. I have therapists who can help them.'"

Diane replied that she didn't know how she would pay for therapy. She wasn't even sure where or how to find her money.

"Don't worry about the money," Scott told her. "We'll take care of it."

Scott had founded an organization that provided therapy for grief-stricken people, especially children, who had experienced a sudden loss, such as death, divorce, abandonment, or incarceration.

People could pay whatever they wished for the therapy.

"If you want to pay a quarter, you pay a quarter," Scott explained. "If you want to pay ten bucks, you pay ten bucks."

The average amount paid per family was $11.80, for a one-hour session that would ordinarily cost hundreds of dollars.

"I don't know where we'd be without Scott Bauer and the foundation," said Diane.

The organization was named the Lauri S. Bauer Foundation for Sudden Loss. Lauri was Scott's late wife. When she died, he wanted to find therapy for his three young boys. He discovered, to his dismay, a scarcity of psychotherapists who specialized in working with grieving children. In his late wife's honor, he founded an organization to help kids like his own.

Lauri Bauer, who was forty-three, had been sitting on the couch with Scott and their three boys, eleven-year-old Brett, thirteen-year-old Jake, sixteen-year-old Alex, and their two dogs, watching a reality show on television, when she remarked that she suddenly didn't feel well.

Scott walked to the kitchen to get her a glass of water. When he returned, she had collapsed. She died before the medics were able to reach the ambulance.

A fitness nut, as Scott described Lauri, she was seemingly in perfect health. She had died of cardiac arrest caused by a sudden arrhythmia, the consequence, they would later learn, of a rare genetic disorder.

A successful options trader, Scott owned a business called Prosper Trading Academy, located in the Chicago Board of Trade, which taught people how to trade options.

An athletic man with close-cropped hair flecked with gray, he was a frequent guest on network financial television shows. Some five years after the death of Lauri, he married a woman named Amy, who had three children of her own, and they formed a blended and loving family.

"It's really important for people to know how lucky I was to have the support of so many people in the community," said Scott. "It's something most people don't have."

Active in his community, Scott had served on the Board of Education for Stevenson High School. In the community youth baseball league, he had held every position, from coach to commissioner, over the course of some twenty-five years.

He said his sons, who witnessed the shocking, sudden death of their mom, benefited greatly from therapy but faced a never-ending struggle to live with the loss, even in the best of times.

He recalled one of his boys hitting a game-winning home run, the kind of thrill that ordinarily would send a kid over the moon. But his son's elation was tempered because every event in life was seen through the prism of his mother's tragic death.

"His reaction was, 'How can I be happy when my mother's gone?'" said Scott. "And I had to remind him that their mother would really, really want him to be happy."

That same advice had also been given many times in the other direction: from the sons to the father.

"The boys," Scott said, "have helped me in that way just as much as I've helped them."

Through therapy, his sons learned that it was okay to open up and talk about feelings of loss and the way it colored their lives.

"And we *do* talk about it—every day," said Scott. "We're an open book."

His sons, Alex, who worked in the restaurant business, and Jake, who worked in finance, both went to Indiana University. The youngest, Brett, who was a recent graduate of the University of Colorado, worked as a political fundraiser in Washington, DC. Brett hoped someday to run for Congress.

He had come a long way from the eleven-year-old boy who felt so lost after the death of his mother.

"I honestly didn't know how I was going to make it another day," Brett recalled. "Every day was hopeless. Like most people in my situation, I thought, 'Why me?' 'Why us?'"

He acknowledged that he had "fought therapy" for years after his mother's death. He would go to the sessions but mostly sit quietly as the therapist talked. While he might not have been saying much, he listened. Things were sinking in. By college, he had come to realize how helpful therapy had been for him.

People who learn about his background have asked what he would say to a young person who has experienced the loss of a parent.

"I'd tell them that it's terrible," he said simply, "but I believe the universe has a way of giving its toughest battles to the toughest soldiers."

After the death of her father, Hannah Shultz, who was eight, emotionally walled herself off, almost unwilling to even acknowledge that her father had died. She did not cry in public but instead went to her bedroom to shed her angry tears. Even on the day of her dad's funeral, she refused to talk about what had happened.

She initially rejected going to therapy. Her mother resorted to bribing her, telling the child she would be given an American Girl doll if she went for at least three sessions.

Hannah took the bait.

"And the more I went to therapy," she said, "the safer a place it seemed to be for me."

Life will never be the same, of course. She still sometimes felt a twinge of envy when she watched friends or other kids sharing experiences with their fathers, even the interactions that weren't so easy. After all, at least they had their dad.

Hannah excelled in many aspects of school and extracurricular life. She was a member of Orchesis and the school dance team. She played on the varsity lacrosse squad. Both she and Max were named to the National Honor Society. They both went to Hebrew school, in part because Jewish tradition and education had been so important to their dad.

She tried extra hard to be a leader, she said, "maybe to fill the void of being left without my leader."

Grief also moved her to be more sensitive to the troubles of other people.

"I try to be kind around everyone," she said, "because you just never know what they're going through."

Max struggled mightily after his father's death. He and his father were extremely close, as much pals as father and son. As his mother put it, "The two of them—they just got each other."

Max and his dad would go camping together and go to ball games whenever they could. They could talk about sports for hours.

At the suggestion of the kids' therapist, Max filled a memory box with memorabilia that evoked his relationship with his dad: a football, some baseball cards, pictures of their favorite professional athletes. He guarded the box as perhaps his most precious possession.

"I could never, ever lose this," he said.

While Hannah tried to hide her grief, Max cried almost constantly for what seemed to be years. Milestones were difficult, like Hannah's bat mitzvah and Max's bar mitzvah, which they marked in a joint ceremony, with a part of the ceremony dedicated to their father.

In youth baseball, Max was drafted by a coach who had been keeping an eye out for him, for reasons that went beyond the game. That coach was Scott Bauer.

"I consider Scott to be one of my role models," Max said, expressing deep gratitude for the counseling he was given. "When I grow up, hopefully I will be successful, and I will donate to Scott's foundation."

Max, like Hannah, excelled in school. His name was on the honor roll. He wrote about sports for the Buffalo Grove High School newspaper, the *Charger*, just as his dad did when he attended that very same school a generation ago. Max played soccer for a couple of years and later performed as a play-by-play commentator for online streaming of the high school's sporting events.

When his father died, Max had told himself he was going to have to grow up fast. As a teenager, he held two jobs, working as a camp counselor (along with his sister), as well as clerking at a local Target store.

He knew finances were going to be a challenge at home, and he vowed to do everything he could to help his mom.

"I like to think that my dad would be proud."

CHAPTER TWENTY-ONE

BLUEPRINTS FOR THE BLIND

As a boy in the church choir, Darin Frerichs sang along with the verses faithfully and enthusiastically. He found it uplifting. But nothing inspired him as much as the woman who played the organ so beautifully.

The organist, Alice, was blind, and so was her husband.

"She amazed me," he said.

Darin also grew up with friends and family members who had lost sight or hearing. His own grandfather had endured hearing loss from World War II, and Darin often worried that someday his grandpa would go entirely deaf. The little boy worried about losing their cherished talks about things like love, respect and understanding.

The years passed quickly, and Darin became the only member of the family to go far in school, first to a community college, then a four-year university, and ultimately, to graduate school. He became an architect.

At his workplace, he learned that a nonprofit organization, the Center for Deaf-Blind Persons, in suburban Milwaukee, was losing its workspace, which had been donated. The nonprofit, which hoped to build its own facility, was looking for an architect willing to oversee blueprints for the project as an unpaid volunteer.

Darin jumped at the chance.

"You just think about being in their shoes," said Darin.

He oversaw the drawings for a new, low-slung building designed with offices that gave teachers and clients more privacy. At four thousand square feet, it was much bigger than the old facility and designed in a way that better fit their needs.

He was there for the opening, and was moved by the show of appreciation.

"They were ecstatic," he said.

The clients at the Center for Deaf-Blind Persons were people like Sam, a fifty-seven-year-old man in a Green Bay Packers cap and a Milwaukee Brewers sweatshirt, who was slowly typing on a Braille-equipped computer, alongside an interpreter, so that he could keep up on the events of the world.

In the nearby cafeteria, meanwhile, Mattie, who was blind, deaf and unable to speak, was eating lunch with the help of a teacher.

As a child, Mattie had been placed in an institution, with strict time limits on how long a meal could last. To keep from going hungry, she would pick up her food with both hands and hurry to cram it in her mouth.

At the Deaf-Blind Center, she learned to eat in a slower, more civil and relaxed manner. She made other advances, too. She got a part-time job at a local school, where she filed paperwork.

When approaching her, a person would reach out to touch her hand, so that she would know someone was nearby. She squeezed the hand and smiled, and then brought the visitor's hand to her cheek, an affectionate gesture to show that she was happy to have company.

The center was founded in 1985 by a remarkable woman named Ruth Silver. In 2012, Ruth wrote a book, using a computer that translated Braille, about her life experiences.

The book began in 1947 when Ruth was sixteen years old, sitting in the back seat of the family's car on the way back from Mayo Clinic, where she had been given a life-changing diagnosis.

Ruth, who had dreams of becoming a cellist in a symphony, had just been told by doctors that she was going blind. In the front seat, she wrote, her mother sat stoically, in denial, while her father sobbed.

After high school, Ruth attended college at what is now the University of Wisconsin–Milwaukee, majoring in exceptional education, with a specialty in teaching deaf children.

When she graduated, she took a job at a school for the deaf in Iowa and then worked at a school for the blind in Massachusetts. She would later return to Milwaukee to marry her college sweetheart, Marvin Silver, a psychiatric social worker. They would soon have a daughter, Julia.

For twelve years, Ruth taught and then directed a school for the blind. But in her early thirties, as she wrote, her "world came crashing down" when she was told by doctors that she was going deaf, too.

A person with the dual conditions, being blind and deaf, has sometimes been described as enduring the heartbreaking experience of "living in dark silence."

Ruth believed that it was a genetic condition. But because her father's family were all killed in the Holocaust, there were no medical records on his side to research.

As her hearing faded, she sank into a terrible depression, unable to rouse herself from bed on some days. The hearing loss gradually worsened.

"The birds finally stopped singing," she later wrote, "and the voices grew muffled."

The love and support of her husband, Marvin, would help pull her through. Marvin would talk to her, and then use touch sign language, tracing letters on her hand to communicate. Before leaving for work each morning, he would tell her:

"I know you'll be up and moving again someday."

Years later, she would write in gratitude about him:

"How fortunate we are to have even one person in our life, a relative or friend, to share our joys and sorrows."

The depths of depression would last about two years. She ultimately became determined to force herself to rejoin the world.

To accomplish her goal, each night before bed she would make a short list of something that *had* to be done the next day, whether it was simply cleaning out the silverware drawer or writing a rough draft of a poem.

It worked.

In 1983, she set out to organize a social and support group of deaf-blind people, along with volunteers, interpreters and supporters. When people lose sight or hearing, they sometimes avoid meeting with friends, fearful that those close to them would feel awkward and drift away. Indeed, that was precisely what sometimes happened.

The group Ruth founded was called WISH (With Impaired Sight-Hearing). People would gather on the first Sunday of the month to share experiences, hopes, fears.

Sometimes they would go on field trips. With the help of a naturalist as a volunteer, as well as interpreters, they took walks through a park, traced the texture of tree bark, experienced the feel and smell of flowers. In the wintertime, they marched through deep drifts of snow before returning home feeling very cold, she wrote, but absolutely exhilarated.

When Ruth came to learn there were no services for deaf-blind people in Milwaukee, she decided to start such a center, drawing on seed money from the Wisconsin Center for the Blind.

Ruth would direct the center as a volunteer. She took no pay.

These days, the center typically worked with about fifty people through the year, all of them with complete or partial loss of the ability to hear and see.

Her goal in starting the center, she would later explain, was to "reduce the extreme isolation and help each person live as independent and fulfilling a life as possible."

She wrote a paper about her mission, which was submitted to a conference of deaf-blind persons at Montclair State College in New Jersey.

It was titled: "Conquering Obstacles: There Are Reasons to Go On."

Ruth did not sugarcoat the challenges or the pain of living without sight or hearing, but she pressed others who shared her circumstances to forge ahead. It was, after all, only the best of the options.

"I wish to say that deaf-blindness is not hopeless," she wrote. "Neither is it easy. At times, you and I have the right to weep, the right to feel angry, the right to feel afraid, and the right to mourn—for surely our losses have been great.

"However, I believe too, that there is much left in life for us to do and enjoy. There are reasons to go on."

At eighty-one, she published a book, *Invisible: My Journey Through Vision and Hearing Loss*. It centered on her physical challenges but ranged across other issues, including bullying, anti-Semitism, even sex.

She wrote the book, she explained, because she wanted people to recognize her issues but also to understand that she and others with blindness and deafness were human beings like others. They just had a steeper hill to climb.

"People ask me how long it takes to adjust to being blind and partially deaf," she told the journalist Meg Kissinger for an article in the *Milwaukee Journal*. "Exactly one lifetime."

Ruth's lifetime ended on September 19, 2017. She was eighty-six. The obituary described her as an "author, teacher and lecturer." To the very end, she was devoted to helping people who were deaf and blind. In lieu of flowers, it was requested that contributions be sent to the Center for Deaf-Blind Persons.

In 2020, Darin Frerichs, the architect, was named president of the board of directors for the center, a volunteer position.

Darin and his wife, Kim, who was also an architect, talked often to their two daughters, who were both in elementary school, about the importance of being kind to others and respectful and understanding of their circumstances.

The girls talked frequently about what it must be like to be blind and deaf. They have even asked Alexa, the wizard inside the computer.

"We have some good table talks," said Darin. "We're big believers in equality, whether it's race, disabilities, you name it. When you cut all the BS, we're all human beings trying to live the best we can."

Darin and Kim have tried to follow the values of a motto they sought to instill in their daughters:

Take less—give more.

CHAPTER TWENTY-TWO

DO I LOOK LIKE THAT?

Every so often, a beleaguered woman in tattered or ill-fitting clothes would wander into Sandy Keller's office in Bloomington, Indiana, desperately searching for a lifeline.

Some of these women were homeless. Others had endured domestic violence. All of them were broke.

They had pushed through the door of Sandy's little business, Ultimate Secretary, thinking it might be a temp agency with an opening for entry-level help, like answering telephones or greeting visitors at a reception desk. But as the owner of a one-woman enterprise, Sandy didn't have any jobs to offer.

It pained her to see people in such straits. Even if a job had been available, however, she knew these women were certainly not "interview ready," as she put it delicately.

In short, nobody was going to give a job to a candidate who wasn't dressed or groomed appropriately for the workplace.

"These women need help," Sandy told a friend in nonprofit circles, agonizing over what she could do for them.

She settled on sponsoring a clothing drive, hoping to collect a relatively small stock of outfits that would be suitable for women in hardship who were looking for a job.

To publicize the drive, the local newspaper, the Bloomington *Herald-Times* donated a small ad space, a two-by-two-inch spot in the classified section, announcing the collection of clothing for struggling women at an upcoming farmers market in town.

On the day of the drive, Sandy wondered: *Will anyone show up?*

They showed up.

"They kept coming and coming and coming," Sandy said. "It seemed like everyone in Bloomington was coming to donate clothes. In five hours, we collected half a semitrailer load—it was a mountain! You couldn't see over the pile of clothes!"

Some of the donated clothes had never been worn. In many cases, the price tags were still attached.

With the abundance of clothing, Sandy decided to open a store, My Sister's Closet, where women would help other women dress for success.

"We're a boutique," Sandy stressed, "not a thrift shop."

The prices were set low, and many of the customers came with a voucher issued by a nonprofit organization, so they would not need to use any money for a purchase.

The store grew so quickly that Sandy needed larger quarters, and not long after, she needed still more space. Eventually, she settled on College Avenue near the campus of Indiana University, in a store with large windows and a black awning over the front entrance.

My Sister's Closet featured attractive business suits, slacks, dresses, blouses and shoes, along with a big supply of undergarments. As Sandy explained, homeless women did not typically have underwear or hygiene products.

In the vast majority of cases, the women had come from harsh and even violent backgrounds, often going back to childhood. Their self-esteem had taken a beating. Sandy was determined to give them a boost.

"When they walk in here," she said, "we want them to know we're cheering for them."

The store relied on a small paid staff and some 450 volunteers, including four interns from Indiana University. For the first handful of years of the store's operation, Sandy took no salary. She eventually drew a very modest paycheck with no benefits.

As the store grew so did its mission. It began to offer guidance in resume and interview prep, as well as instruction in consumer math and life skills. All of those services were free.

Mary Wheeler, who wore threadbare clothes, walked into My Sister's Closet one afternoon. She had long ago resigned herself to a life of never-ending turmoil.

As a child growing up in a rural Indiana town of six hundred people, she had endured abusive treatment from her father. At seventeen, she became pregnant and was kicked out of her high school.

Without a high school diploma, most employment doors were closed to her. She had mostly worked in housekeeping and food services in nursing homes, at meager wages.

Mary married an older man who was "not very good to me," she said, but she put up with his dehumanizing treatment because she did not want to disrupt the lives of her children.

"When you're used to physical abuse, you just let it go," she said. "You don't want to upset the kids by leaving."

After their house burned, she finally decided to leave him and moved with her teenage children to Bloomington.

Mary was overweight, struggling with depression, and so lacking in confidence that she could scarcely make eye contact. She had endured two strokes and severe arthritis. She had undergone forty-two surgeries for various ailments and injuries.

"When I went on interviews, they told me I just didn't have the 'right look' for the job," she said. "In other words, I was old, fat and ugly."

A counselor sent her to My Sister's Closet, and she experienced the kind of acceptance she had never known before.

"A volunteer in the store wrapped her arms around me," Mary recalled about the first day she walked into the place, "and she just said to me, 'It's going to be okay.'"

Mary walked out of the store that day with some smart new suits. As she steadily gained confidence, she landed a position as an assistant manager in retail. She later secured what she described as her dream job: a peer mentor at a mental health center. She soon qualified for certification as a health coach. She worked with clients on smoking cessation and maintenance of diabetes among other issues.

As her life improved, she returned to My Sister's Closet, asking if they could use her as a volunteer. This time, she would be the person helping the brittle lost souls who came to the store for help. It gave her a sense of meaning and purpose that lifted her spirits.

"The more you give back," Mary said, "the better life becomes."

One morning, Mary noticed a young woman who had come into the store pushing a stroller. The woman held a voucher in her hands but stared at the floor, as if she was too frightened to talk.

Mary thought to herself: *I know that feeling.*

The young woman finally summoned the nerve to speak.

"I have a voucher," she said. "But I don't know if I deserve to use it."

Wheeler asked, "Why on earth not?"

In a voice heavy with shame, the woman explained that she had lost a child, a small boy. The woman said her former husband, in a rage, had thrown the boy across the room against a wall. Her son died from the injuries.

Her husband went to prison. And the guilt-ridden young mother went to the streets.

"I didn't protect my son," she said. "I don't deserve anything."

She and a little daughter were staying at a homeless shelter, where someone had encouraged her to visit My Sister's Closet.

Mary, who was in her early sixties, listened to the younger woman, then nodded in the direction of the little girl in the stroller.

"Doesn't she deserve a better life than you've had?" she asked.

The young mother, in a voice that barely rose over a whisper, answered without reservation.

"Absolutely."

Mary gave her some unvarnished advice.

"Well, if *you* don't have a better life, it's going to be very hard for *her* to have one," she told the young woman.

Mary pushed the stroller as the woman tried on clothes. When the young mom came out of the dressing room wearing a pretty outfit, she glimpsed at the mirror in astonishment.

"Do I really look like that?" she asked.

"You do," Mary assured her.

With her new clothes, the young mom pushed the stroller out of the door. About two weeks later, she returned.

This time, her head was held high.

"I got a job," she announced.

The position was at Indiana University. The pay was decent. And the job came with benefits.

"We have an apartment now," she said, with a note of triumph. "And I have a baby bed and a high chair. I could have no other furniture at all—and I'd be happy."

Months passed, and the young mom returned to the store once again.

"Come outside," she told the volunteers at the store. "I've got something to show you."

In a parking space, there was an automobile—albeit an old model with some rust and more than a few dents.

"I know it's not the best," she acknowledged, "but it's mine!"

As she recounted the scene, Mary's eyes grew shiny.

"This was a girl who learned that she really did deserve something," she said. "And she went from zero to go!"

As for herself, Mary had found her place in the world, and even the occasional miracle, as she put it, in her work at My Sister's Closet.

Mary lost quite a bit of weight. She was donning a stylish scarf, some fashionable shoes, attractive dress slacks, and matching turquoise necklace and earrings.

She had also found companionship in a roommate, a woman who was also in her sixties.

"I live on $734 a month," she said, "but we make it work."

They spend their days growing tomatoes, watching movies, and checking on one another's health.

"I'm living my best life," she said. "I'm such a happy girl."

CHAPTER TWENTY-THREE

SITTING AROUND LIKE A TOAD

Hal Stevenson, who lived in a retirement home in Des Moines, leaned over and spoke in a kind of conspiratorial whisper.

"Don't get me wrong, there's nothing wrong with old people," said Hal, who was in his mid-eighties himself. "But the constant talk about ailments—the complaining and the moaning and the groaning…"

He shook his head.

Hal said he was not about to spend the rest of his days sitting around, illustrating his aches and pains, and droning on about his latest doctor reports with fellow codgers.

A retired agricultural feed company worker and a widower, Hal had always prided himself on pulling his weight and trying to contribute to the lives of those who haven't had an easy way. He and his late wife, Judy, had taken in ten foster children over the years. The last one came to them when he was thirteen. He recently turned sixty-six.

"He was family on the day that he came, and he's family to this day," said Hal. "He's in my will."

Now, at this stage of his life, Hal needed to find a stronger reason to get up and get going every day.

"I was struggling," he said. "I'm a positive person, but I was just sitting around like a toad. I thought, 'I've got to do something. Maybe I could be a volunteer.'"

He was familiar with the Des Moines YMCA Supportive Housing Campus, which utilized an unusual and holistic approach to help sustain, fortify and train people who faced adversity and ended up homeless.

These were displaced veterans, survivors of domestic abuse, the disabled, young people who had been rejected by parents over sexual or gender issues, people who lost businesses in the pandemic, those with a history of mental health problems and addiction.

Hal made a call to the program and asked if a fellow like him could possibly be of any use to them.

He explained it would need to be "a sit-down job," as he put it, since he had trouble with his legs.

The response was immediate:

"Absolutely!"

For a year now, Hal had been working as a YMCA volunteer in a tiny office in the gleaming three-story campus, incongruously set in a gritty Des Moines neighborhood on the site of an old jail that had been demolished.

He devoted himself to whatever task was needed at the moment, right down to sorting donated toothbrushes and dental floss and putting them into packets for each of the residents.

"We are not a homeless shelter," said Brooke Heldt, the program's community engagement director. "We are a hand up, not a handout. And we're not holding their hand. We're walking alongside them."

Each resident lived in one of the 140 efficiency apartments and paid $540 in rent, or fifteen percent of their wages or benefits, whichever was less.

Residents were offered training for employment skills and computer literacy, given advice about securing independent living, offered counseling for personal issues, and provided access to laundry machines.

They were expected to buy and prepare food in their apartments, except for the home-cooked dinner that was served every Tuesday.

To finance the program, the center relied on the rent payments of residents, as well as corporate and civic donors, and the generosity of ordinary people who contributed staples for everyday living, like the toothbrushes that Hal was sorting.

Some of the clients had lived on the campus for years. Others were back on their feet in six months, working jobs and renting their own apartments. The graduates of the program worked in security, construction, restaurants, warehouses, or even started their own businesses.

About 80 percent of the clients were men. They ranged in age from early twenties to eighty-nine. Some 50 percent were veterans, including some who were mistreated in the military for being gay.

"As a queer woman myself," said Brooke, a young Iowa native with a captivating charm, "I can connect with them."

Brooke said the clients at the supportive housing center were a diverse group in seemingly every way—age, race, education level. There was a strong bond of community, she said, perhaps born of adversity.

"Those who have been through the hardest things," said Brooke, "are often the most accepting people."

Unlike the atmosphere at some social service facilities, the YMCA program was intent on avoiding being patronizing or condescending. The clients were treated as adults capable of making their own decisions.

The campus was dry, but if a client came home after having stopped at a bar, they were not reprimanded.

"They're adults," said Brooke. "If they want to go somewhere and have a few beers, who are we to say anything? Now if they're clearly intoxicated, we'd tell them to go to their apartment and sleep it off."

If they were a danger to themselves or others, of course, steps could be taken to end their residency.

"But we're not looking to evict people," said Brooke.

Shawn Carpenter, a square-shouldered fifty-three-year-old man in a green IBEW union shirt—a gift from his nephew, an electrician—sat down in the cafeteria with a blueberry muffin and a plastic glass filled with lemonade.

"I lost my job at a factory and became homeless," he said simply. "That's how I ended up here."

Almost completely deaf from birth, he depended on hearing aids. Even then, hearing was a struggle. On jobs that required vigorous manual labor, sweat would drip into his ears, which could ruin the hearing devices. But he couldn't take them out, or he would risk being reprimanded by a boss who needed him to be able to hear instructions, or the sound of a nearby forklift.

Like many people who grew up with hearing loss, Shawn had a speech impediment, which made him a frequent target of ridicule.

"I've been bullied all of my life," he said. "That's why I don't really like to be around people."

With the help of counselors at the YMCA center, he was able to get better hearing aids and receive training to speak more clearly. He had also received counseling about managing anger issues, which he attributed to being teased about the way he spoke.

"It's an ongoing battle, but the counselor is helping me feel more comfortable around people," said Shawn. "This place helps individuals who want to be helped."

Shawn was especially appreciative of people like Hal, who went out of their way to show kindness.

"Sometimes they'll ask to sit down with you and ask how you're doing, how you're feeling," he said. "Even just having a familiar face say hi, that makes you feel good."

Like the other clients, Shawn received occasional notes of encouragement from Hal.

"I'll write a little note that says, 'We like you and we're glad you're here,'" said Hal. "And I'll draw a big heart. It's a pick-me-up for the residents. At least, I hope it is."

It has not only been a benefit for the residents. Hal said the experience has brought deeper meaning to his own life.

"When you see people who you know are struggling and you can put a smile on their face," said Hal, trying hard to choke back tears, "it just makes you feel so good."

Brooke stepped into the office and gave Hal a hug.

"He's like another grandpa to me," she said, growing a bit teary-eyed herself.

CHAPTER TWENTY-FOUR

A GUY WITH A CHAIN SAW

By his estimate, Brian Tindall has picked up more than nine thousand pounds of trash from woods and waterways in Los Angeles County.

Wearing a cap, bandanna and a "Save the Locals" t-shirt, Brian, whose regular job was working as an electrician in the entertainment business, had never been paid a cent for his cleanup efforts.

"In the larger scheme of things, one person picking up trash is maybe not that big of a deal," he said. "But for the one fish or animal that now is not going to choke to death on a Styrofoam cup, it means everything."

At seven o'clock in the morning on a blazing Sunday in the urban wilderness of the Peck Road Water Reclamation Park near the town of Arcadia, he was hard at it again—clad in gloves and long sleeves as protection from thorns and whatever kind of crud he might encounter.

His motivation for launching his volunteer mission, which he began about three years earlier, was simple:

"I wanted to clean the ocean."

The water in Peck Park eventually makes its way to the Los Angeles River, and ultimately to the Pacific Ocean, which had long been fouled by trash tossed aside by humans. What is known as the Great Pacific Garbage Patch, an infamously polluted stretch of the sea, is said to be six feet deep in plastic, some 1.8 trillion pieces of detritus.

A lean, bearded thirty-six-year-old with an easy laugh, Brian referred to himself as "an environmental weirdo." He once talked a demolition crew of guys in hard hats into rerouting a driveway for a Chick-fil-A in order to save a thirty-foot sycamore tree. He has also started a local community garden and he began growing milkweed for monarch butterflies, an endangered species. He chose Peck Park as a site to clean, in part because it was only about a half mile from his home, which meant using little gas and emitting less carbon.

Brian has pulled all kinds of things from the woods and water—an ottoman, kayaks, logs, tires. He has retrieved seven shopping carts from the shallow lake, as well as a huge tire that was once presumably attached to a semitrailer. The biggest piece he has recovered was a massive cable spool.

"I have no idea in the world how it got there," he said.

Using a rope, he dragged the big spool up a hillside—where it tipped over more than once—and pulled it more than one hundred feet to the dumpster where he would leave his recovered garbage. It took four hours. The Arcadia Public Works crew would later come by to empty the dumpster.

"There is great satisfaction in getting the big stuff," he said. "It's something tangible."

He was also intrigued by coming across historical artifacts, like the empty bag of Doritos from 1992 he snagged one recent morning.

Besides hauling out junk, he trimmed trees, pulled weeds, and sprinkled seed. He took three days to rip out the rampant growth of castor beans, a non-native species that was crowding out the natural plants that feed insects and facilitate a healthy ecosystem.

His drive to make a difference, he believed, might be handed down by example. His father was a nurse who advised young men how to avoid the draft during the Vietnam War era. His dad, a volunteer firefighter, also spent spare time picking up trash. His mother, a physician, had provided care for people in New Zealand and Nicaragua as a member of Doctors Without Borders.

Peck Park, with the magnificent San Gabriel Mountains in the distance, occupied land that was formerly an alluvial pebble quarry. The lake was formed as a shallow basin when the Army Corps channeled the San Gabriel and Rio Hondo Rivers.

Over the decades, the park and lake have undergone a slow transformation from a barren, postindustrial quarry landscape to a nature setting for bird-watching, biking, hiking and running trails.

It was also popular as a place for homeless encampments, as well as a relatively discreet site for meth labs.

"I have zero problem with the homeless," Brian said. "I do have a problem with the trash."

Brian had carried a taser gun for protection ever since an unleashed dog charged at him, growling with teeth bared, and circled him until the owner came along.

As he was trimming trees in the park, he drew attention from a squinty-eyed sheriff's deputy, who wondered what in the world he was up to.

"I don't blame him," said Brian. "A guy walking around with a chain saw, after all, is going to arouse some suspicion."

When he explained his mission, the law man nodded with admiration, and handed him his business card.

"If you ever have any trouble," he told Brian, "give me a call."

He occasionally got words of thanks from the fishermen or other regulars at the park, many of them retirees and people on disability who came to sit and enjoy the sunshine and perhaps sip a few beers.

He had frequently asked friends and acquaintances to join him in his work. He has gotten no takers.

"I put up a post about coming out here and I get fourteen 'likes' and six people say they are going to come and help," he said. "But then nobody shows up. This is not exactly what people find fun."

Even his wife, Casey Carlson, turned him down.

"I once tried to save a bee and it nearly killed me," he said. "That's my wife's favorite story about what an idiot I am."

He believes she was just teasing.

"Actually, she thinks I'm adorable."

Weary and sweaty after hours of hunting for garbage, Brian surveyed the scene. There was still plenty of work to be done.

"Trash—there's so much of it," he said, with a groan of disgust. "Look! Cups, bottles, cans."

He tried to look on the positive side.

"I guess if there wasn't so much trash, I wouldn't have a project."

When he finally called it a day, he climbed into his compact Honda, a vehicle he jokingly called the Murder Mobile, nicknamed for the suspicious materials inside.

"I've got a shovel, ropes, trash bags," he said. "If I get pulled over, I'm in trouble."

CHAPTER TWENTY-FIVE

PRIDE AFTER DISGRACE

Growing up the son of a butcher in a working-class town, not far from the old steel mills, the successes of Mark McCombs inspired a lot of local pride.

He had made his way to prestigious Northwestern University Law School, where he graduated first in his class, and then went on to a highly respected legal career, rising to become a partner at a big firm.

People in the hardscrabble village of Calumet Park, south of Chicago, were so proud of their brilliant native son that they named a street after him.

He was living proof that someone from a humble beginning could compete with the best and the brightest. As a big-shot lawyer, he even came home to help.

Mark represented Calumet Park in a project aimed at rejuvenating the struggling town using Tax Increment Financing, better known as TIF, for commercial investment on the very street that bore his name.

And then he got busted.

He was charged with bilking his hometown, fraudulently billing $500 an hour for work he had not done.

"No two ways about it, what I did was wrong," he said. "I stole from my client."

At fifty-three, he was convicted of theft and sent to an Illinois state prison. He lost his freedom, his job, his wife, his money, his law license, and his reputation. And he became estranged from his four kids.

"If I had to pick one thing," he said, "being estranged from the kids—that's the hardest."

In prison, he worked to take an inventory of himself and address the ways his life had gone off track.

"My addiction was to pride and prestige," he said. "Money was the way to get to those things. I could go back to my hometown and think, 'Hey, look at me now.'"

After the arrest and news of his wrongdoing went public, most of his friends and colleagues seemed to disappear.

In lockup, he bonded with people who came from a world apart from elite corporate law but who shared with him a kinship that transcended college diplomas and bank accounts.

"You find out really quickly who your real friends are," he said. "It becomes a kind of blessing in disguise. And you appreciate relationships so much more when you need to lean on someone."

When he was released from prison, he came to learn that reentry to society, in many ways, could be more difficult than incarceration itself.

"In prison, you're in there with like-minded people, you get a lot of support and there's a feeling that 'we're all in this together,'" he said.

"And then you finish your sentence and you think you should be square with the house. But you're not. It's like you're branded with a kind of scarlet letter."

Many of those who are released end up going back to prison. Some don't survive. Mark's friend, Clint, who was struggling to find a foothold after being released, ultimately turned a gun on himself in an alley in downtown Chicago and ended his life. After Mark posted words of sympathy on Facebook, some people trolled with online comments that a coldhearted criminal like Clint didn't deserve any kind words.

"What he did was wrong," said Mark. "But at the end of the day, we are all somebody's son or daughter, somebody's friend."

After leaving prison, Mark worked in kitchens for five years, first at restaurants and later as a cook at a college fraternity. He ultimately landed a job as a policy analyst with the Safer Foundation, an organization that worked on ways to improve the transition from prison.

He volunteered for a new organization called the Illinois Alliance for Reentry and Justice, helping to devise a structure and plan for the group.

He also created a webinar, "Know Your Rights," which was streamed directly into prisons, offering tips about navigating life after leaving prison. It focused on challenges like obtaining a driver's license, finding housing, understanding the status of voting eligibility, taking steps to expunge a criminal record.

He delivered talks to men who were on work release, sometimes at a gathering at a Salvation Army. These were men, many of them worried about the coming transition, who were yearning to hear encouraging words about the future.

"There *is* life on the other side," Mark would tell them. "You're going to be okay."

He could look in their eyes and see that he was making an impact. For Mark, a man who had done wrong, lost everything, and endured public disgrace, it was a way to give back.

It made him feel proud.

"I'd leave those presentations feeling three inches taller."

CHAPTER TWENTY-SIX

LIVING IN FEAR

On the domestic violence hotline, Chris Riedl listened as a woman explained why she got smacked around by her husband.

"I didn't cook his dinner the way he likes it," the woman told Chris. "That's why he hit me."

In her time volunteering as a counselor, Chris had heard almost every excuse, rationalization, and defense of a partner's abusive behavior.

"Many of them second-guess themselves," she said. "The abuse is somehow their fault. Their self-esteem is so low. They're told by the abuser, 'You can't do anything right,' and they hear it so often that they actually come to believe it."

They have been told that they are ugly, fat, stupid, that nobody likes them, and that even their own parents have bad-mouthed them, which was almost certainly a lie.

Many times, Chris has been told: "He thinks I'm having an affair."

Her response: "Even if you *were* having an affair, that doesn't justify abuse."

The counseling hotline was operated by a domestic violence shelter that provided refuge to women and their children. The shelter would also help instruct callers about how to file for an order of protection or to be referred to emergency counseling.

The ages of those who called for help and guidance, Chris said, ranged from eighteen to eighty.

As Chris had come to learn, the physical, emotional or financial abuse tended to boil down to a desire for power and control. Many of the callers to the hotline said they were not permitted to spend time with anyone if the husband or partner was not present. Many of these women often had no social life, no friends.

It was not uncommon for an abuser to threaten to take the children away "and you'll never see them again." Chris knew of some cases where women were beaten so severely they ended up in a hospital. And yet, many refused medical treatment or declined to cooperate with the police.

Sometimes the battered woman would call the hotline from a car. In some cases, after a terrified woman had finally fled the abuser, she was actually living in a car.

"But some of our callers don't have a vehicle," said Chris. "They don't have a job. They don't have a bank account. They have been stripped of any power."

Chris has even worked with expectant women whose partners grew jealous because the pregnancy had taken too much attention and left them feeling ignored.

The calls to the hotline would come when the abuser was not around. In those cases where the abuser was in the house, the callers usually spoke furtively, sometimes whispering that they were in a locked room.

Chris would ask a series of yes–no questions:
Is the abuser near you?
Has the abuser hurt you?
Will he?
Would you like me to call the police?

Chris would tell each caller that the discussion was confidential, with three exceptions: if there was evidence of child abuse, if the victim was over age sixty, or if the person being threatened or abused was considering harming themselves.

The hotline volunteer would not explicitly tell the caller what to do. The abused person had likely already been bullied and demeaned so severely that she had lost much sense of control or agency. Chris said it was important to let her make the decisions.

Despite a myth that domestic violence was predominantly a problem among working-class or low-income people, Chris said, the cases crossed every social and demographic category, from janitors to judges. Indeed, it was often more challenging to call out the abuse when the abuser was a prominent figure in the community.

"He's a big executive in his company," more than one woman has told Chris. "He has money." "He's so popular. Everyone likes him." "No one will believe me."

In many instances, one parent would tell the children such terrible things about the other parent that it harmed their relationship. Indeed, that was the intent.

Some of the abusers engaged in gaslighting, acting as though their partner was just imagining that anything was wrong. Some of these psychological abusers would move furniture and other items around the house so that the partner believed she was losing her mind.

Most callers to the domestic violence hotline were women—but not all of them.

"Believe it or not, there are abusive women out there, too," said Chris. "But men are less likely to call."

In cases of same-sex couples, especially when the target of abuse was closeted, there would be threats of outing.

"I'm going to let everyone know you're gay. I'm going to post it on social media."

Those who were undocumented immigrants faced special risks.

"I'm going to tell the authorities that you're illegal and not even supposed to be in this country."

Chris, who also volunteered as a CASA advocate for abused and neglected children, had once held a post with a major insurance company. She now volunteered for the domestic violence hotline two mornings a week.

"The system is broken," she said. "We let our survivors down. There is a lot to be done in education in our society to let survivors know they have their rights."

For Chris, it was wrenching to hear such anguish in the voices of callers who were being threatened or abused.

It stirred painful memories.

"I had a situation where I was experiencing some of these things," she said, "and I was given help and support, so it was my turn to give back."

Chris was now fifty-five, happily remarried, and the mother of two sons. But when she was in her early twenties, she lived with a man she came to fear.

She was not permitted to be with friends or family. He falsely accused her of outlandish behavior. When she finally left him, he would stalk her, driving around her apartment building at night, circling the block again and again. She changed the locks on her apartment.

In the parking lot outside a restaurant, Chris was having a casual conversation with a male acquaintance when her husband pulled up. He burst out of his car and physically attacked the man.

It was clear she had to sever ties with her husband, but it was not an easy step to take.

"For a long time, I second-guessed myself," she said. "I grew up Catholic and I would be the first person in my family to get divorced."

As it turned out, her parish priest was very supportive. Chris ultimately moved out of the state.

"And I was lucky," she said. "I didn't own a home with him, I didn't have children with him. It was not the really tangled mess a lot of people have to deal with."

Recounting the memories, she trembled with emotion.

"All these years later," she said tearfully, "it's still very difficult to talk about."

She looked back at those experiences with a surprising degree of understanding. She had let go of anger. She hoped that her former husband had gotten help.

"It was learned behavior," she said. "He thought as long as he wasn't cheating, he was a good husband."

She described her current husband as loving, kind and trusting. One of their sons was a teenager; the other was in his early twenties. She had told both of them everything about her first husband, hoping to underscore his behavior "as an example of how not to treat women."

Chris was determined that her sons would grow up with a healthier view of relationships and the rights of women.

She has told them:

"Women are equals. They need to be treated with respect. They have a right to make their own decisions."

It was largely the same message she conveyed to those who called the hotline, women who had been falsely told through words or actions that they were powerless. In her volunteer work, Chris was determined to change that narrative.

"If I can move the needle just a little bit," she said, "that's what I want to do."

CHAPTER TWENTY-SEVEN

ALMOST HOME

Just before her graduation from high school, Sarah O'Malley learned she was going to have a baby. Single and pregnant at seventeen, she did not go off to college, as so many of her peers were able to do. Instead, she took two low-paying jobs to support herself and, soon, her baby boy.

When her son was two, she was working as a dental assistant and as a waitress in an Italian restaurant, where she noticed a cook, a handsome young immigrant who did not speak English.

"I told my parents that night: 'I met a young man and I don't know his name and I don't know where he is from—but I know that I am going to marry him.'"

Her mother and father simply laughed.

Sarah and the young cook, Adrian Galvan, who had come from Mexico City, would indeed fall in love, and several months later, after she became pregnant, they began planning their wedding.

She had found a job she loved, working with adults with Down syndrome. Adrian was working for a granite installation company. They saved enough to buy a 900-square-foot home, one-half of a modest duplex, in a community called Hometown, just south of Chicago.

Their little home would grow very cozy as a third baby arrived, and then a fourth, and a fifth.

There was no shortage of love in the home, but money was another matter. Sarah and Adrian were earning barely enough to make ends meet. And then financial disaster struck. The economy tanked, and they both lost their jobs in a matter of a couple of weeks.

They desperately searched for ways to survive. Every evening, they would load their young children into their truck and go scavenging through garbage bins, looking for anything Adrian could clean, fix and sell—a vacuum, a microwave, tools, toys.

"And on Sundays, we'd all go to the Swap-o-Rama," she said, "and sell other people's garbage to feed our children."

Sarah and Adrian sold every personal belonging they could—even their wedding rings.

It wasn't enough.

The power company shut off the electricity. The kids did their homework by candlelight.

Ultimately, the home went into foreclosure. Two days before the bank was scheduled to kick them out, Sarah went to the mailbox, which was stuffed with a large stack of bills. In the middle was a white envelope with her name but no return address.

She opened it and found a cashier's check—a sum large enough to save the house. To this day, it remains a mystery to Sarah who sent the money.

Overcome with gratitude, she vowed that she would devote her life to helping people in distress, especially the homeless.

To get their personal finances straightened out, she and Adrian, a talented fix-it man, started a business, Handy Andy's Home Improvement, specializing in remodeling kitchens and bathrooms.

And then Sarah went to work helping those in need. She would name her rescue venture Almost Home.

With barely a clue of what the process entailed, she googled: "*How to start a nonprofit organization.*"

It turned out to be a bit more complicated than she might have thought.

The site listed fourteen steps, including a mission statement, the establishment of a board of directors, the filing of paperwork for 501(c)(3) status for tax-exempt standing, and the publication of articles of incorporation.

There was also the matter of finances.

Starting a nonprofit, she learned, required money. While Adrian's business was keeping the family afloat, it wasn't as if there were piles of extra cash lying around.

Sarah would not be deterred. She would go out and beg for the seed money.

She fashioned a sign:

"I am not homeless," it read, "but I am on a mission to help those who are."

She walked the streets, and walked and walked, asking strangers to contribute to her cause. After sixteen months of panhandling, she had raised $1,200, enough to incorporate Almost Home. A friend, the mother of a classmate of one of her children, was a lawyer and volunteered to file the 501(c)(3) paperwork.

Almost Home was born.

Operating out of her home, Sarah would walk daily to search for the homeless, determined to straighten out their circumstances.

"In my naïve way, I thought I would just talk to homeless people and fix their problems, and everything would be all better."

As she came to learn, it wasn't quite so simple.

"Their problems are not mine to fix," she said. "That's between them and 'the man upstairs.' It's not my place to change them but to meet them where they are."

In her daily walk to find the homeless, she carried a bottle of water, a soda pop, a cup of coffee.

"Hi, my name is Sarah," she would introduce herself, "I brought this for you."

That would serve as an icebreaker that led to a discussion about their lives and needs. Sarah would take note of their circumstances. When she got home, she would log on to social media to publicize her mission and call out to potential donors.

"My friend Anthony needs a pair of shoes," she posted. "Would you like to buy him some?"

And someone would.

"My friend Steve needs his phone bill paid. Would you like to pay it for him?"

And someone stepped up.

The homeless people she helped were never described as "clients" or "guests." Sarah simply called them her friends.

In her appeals to donors, she knew some people might be skeptical. So she always gave them the option of sending the money to her, and she would take care of the purchase, or sending it directly to a business in the name of the person in need.

Word of her campaign spread, and her social media following grew. Over and over, donors would answer her pleas. They sent money for food, socks, underwear, sleeping bags, blankets.

Sarah took the offerings to the homeless, who she found often were living beneath bridges.

Talk of her work got around on the streets, too.

"You're Sarah Galvan," one man greeted her with a smile. "I've been waiting for you."

Sarah would become known among the homeless as "Our Mother of the Bridges."

For six years, she worked the phones and computer out of her home, where she stacked supplies for the homeless.

Along the way, she had babies six and seven. And her mission continued to grow. The small half-duplex, as home to a rescue headquarters and a big family, finally reached its limit.

"There would be homeless friends at the kitchen table, homeless friends on the couch, babies everywhere, people showing up in the wee hours," she said. "This was not sustainable."

She needed space. So Sarah headed out to churches to ask if they could spare a small office and room for a weekly soup kitchen.

"Twenty-two churches heard my request," she said, "and twenty-two churches said 'No.'"

They all said she was doing the Lord's work, of course, and that they wished her nothing but the best.

"But they didn't want *those people here*," she said. "I heard it over and over and over. *Not here. Not here. Not here.* We don't want *those people* in *our* church."

Sarah was a religious person, though she was not baptized until her thirties. She was raised by supportive parents who were committed atheists. Her own mother had felt the lash of disapproval from a religious body. At sixteen, she had become pregnant and was kicked out of her Catholic high school.

Disappointed by the unwelcoming stance of so many churches—and well aware that many homeless people felt unwelcome in places of worship—Sarah grew resigned to the possibility that there might be no room available at any religious inn.

And then she decided to give it one more try. She reached out to the Alive Church in Oak Lawn, Illinois.

"And they bought my crazy idea of a soup kitchen," she said, "and they even gave me an office."

It was not a glamorous spread. The room for the soup kitchen was in the basement of the church. Her drafty office, where she stored staples for the homeless, like socks and underwear, was a level below the basement. In other words, as Sarah put it, "It's in the basement of the basement."

She worked in the office space from nine o'clock in the morning until three o'clock in the afternoon every weekday while her kids were at school. Dinner for the homeless—and anyone else who needed it—was served on Saturday and Tuesday evenings. Her husband, Adrian, and the children would usually come to help serve food to the homeless.

Sarah's homeless friends often struggled with opioid addiction and mental health problems.

"But the majority of my friends are alcoholics."

Almost Home did not turn away people who showed up after they had been drinking, as some shelters and soup kitchens do.

For those who decided to go to rehab, Sarah would arrange for transportation. If they entered a sober house, she would send care packages with everything from blankets to sweets.

"It's important that they know someone is rooting for them," she said.

Sarah had lost many of her homeless friends. She carried Narcan, the antidote for opioid overdoses, at all times. She had used the medication to save the life of one of her friends, Joe, although the man would later die of a subsequent overdose.

In her office, she kept photographs of Joe and several other friends who were gone.

"There's Billy," she pointed to the portrait of a young man who died of AIDS at twenty-four. "He was gay and his parents shunned him."

Sarah distributed gas cards to people living in dilapidated vans and cars. They weren't necessarily traveling, but they needed to start their vehicles every few hours in the winter to keep from freezing.

On the Saturday before Christmas, the friends of Sarah gathered at the soup kitchen for dinner. For many of them, it would be the only real meal they would have all week.

The folding tables were filled with barbecued chicken, macaroni and cheese, pasta, french toast casserole, meatballs, bread and salad.

Some of Sarah's donors had made the food themselves and brought it to the kitchen. Others paid to have food catered.

Most of the homeless diners were men, although there were some women, including a young immigrant mother who was holding a baby in her arms.

In the church basement that night, many of the homeless had gotten more than just food from her.

A forty-year-old man named Michael, rail-thin and bearded, hunched over a plate of mostaccioli and meatballs. A former trucker who had lost his job, he was living on the street when he met Sarah.

"I was in a very dark place," he said. "She's helped me stay warm, and my dog, too. People tell me I should get rid of the dog because she's expensive. But I won't, because she's my only family."

She used donations to buy him an old van, where he was staying until he earned enough money from his new job as a forklift operator—also arranged by Sarah—to be able to rent an apartment.

Kyel, who was thirty-five, became homeless after he lost his job at a food distributor when it was shut down by the health department. He had a brother in Utah, but Kyel had three children living in Chicago with their mother, and he wanted to be around them. He had not told his kids that he was living in an old van, or that he had slept under bridges before Sarah came to the rescue.

"I don't want them to worry about things they can't control," he said.

He had felt overwhelmed by life. He couldn't even renew his driver's license because, as a homeless person, he didn't have an address.

"I gave Sarah a call and told her I was desperate," he said.

She told him:

"Come in here. We'll figure it out."

Scott Duignan, who was in his sixties, was a former carpenter who fell on hard times and became homeless.

"I got this coat from Sarah," he said, pointing to the blue down jacket he was wearing. "Sarah is amazing. With her, there is absolutely no judgment."

Our Mother of the Bridges, as the homeless called her, had experienced judgment and shame, but she had also known the kindness of a stranger. She was determined to repay it.

CHAPTER TWENTY-EIGHT

FRIDAY IS TIE DAY

As a mentor at a teen center in southern New Jersey, Darrell Edmonds was prepping a young man for a job interview, when he asked him what he was going to wear to the meeting.

"Oh, I thought a button-up shirt," the teenager told Edmonds.

"No tie?" Darrell asked.

"I don't have a tie," the young man explained.

Darrell took off his own tie and handed it to him.

"I don't know how to tie it," the teen confessed.

Darrell taught the young man how to wrap the tie and fashion a knot.

The next day, two more young men came to his office with the same predicament. The day after that, five more showed up.

In many of these cases, Darrell realized, the young men lived in homes without a father or another male figure who could teach them how to fasten a tie, among so many other lessons.

The experience inspired Darrell to volunteer to start a mentoring organization called Friday Is Tie Day.

He encouraged the young men to wear business attire on Fridays as a way to stand out. It would show they were serious about their ambitions.

"For young men of color, the bar is often low," said Darrell, a Black man. "A lot of these kids were being left behind. Not much was expected of them. But they had potential."

Friday Is Tie Day would grow into something of a support group. Under Darrell's tutelage, the group of South Jersey adolescents would meet once a week at a local pizzeria to talk about their future plans, and whatever else was on their minds: dating lives, family relationships, ways to become effective leaders, the importance of ethical manhood.

The organization would expand its reach to forty Black and Latino males from a dozen middle schools and high schools. Darrell began to make appearances at schools to explain the values of the group and to seek out boys who could benefit from mentoring and brotherhood.

"There are few things that bring me this much joy," said Darrell, a fortyish man with a charismatic presence. "I literally get a high when I'm being productive with these guys. There's no feeling like it."

Like many of the members of Friday Is Tie Day, Daylen Carson didn't quite know what to expect when he first attended a gathering of the group.

"My mother found out about it on Facebook," said Daylen, a student at Oakcrest High School in Mays Landing, New Jersey. "I didn't want to join. I'm not a social person. But my mom kind of pushed me. She said, 'Just try it out.'"

Daylen, who "tries my best to stay in touch with my father," soon found that he drew strength and wisdom from Darrell and the fellow members of the Friday Is Tie Day group.

"I fell in love with it," he said. "It turned out to be the best organization I've ever been part of. It was an opportunity to grow up and learn about true manhood—being a leader, a worker, a provider. Being a man means being there. It's about keeping your promises."

For Darrell, those were the lessons he said he had learned from his own devoted father, Jesse, a social worker and church deacon who died in 2014, and his steadfast uncles. He felt a desire to pass along the wisdom that had been handed down to him.

Going through high school in Egg Harbor City, New Jersey, Edmonds had been a top student and a star football player, good enough to win a scholarship to the University of Delaware, where he was a linebacker and a captain on the team.

As enriching as football was for him, Darrell believed that too much emphasis was put on sports—one of the only endeavors where he believed society expected great things from young Black men—and not enough attention was given to academic potential and leadership gifts.

He organized a College Decision Day ceremony each spring at Rowan University in Glassboro, New Jersey, to honor the graduating seniors and celebrate with families.

If Darrell seemed like he was doing seven things at once, that's because he usually was.

On a Sunday morning in early June, hours before the ceremony at Rowan would begin, he was hustling around so swiftly to get things ready that he broke a sweat.

He organized picnic tables on a brick patio under canopies near the school's library. He took calls to give directions to the gathering spot. He checked on the DJ. He helped assemble portraits of the seniors in easels. In a Hollywood touch, a red carpet was laid, leading to the visages of each of the college-bound students being honored.

For the big celebration, younger members of the organization were invited, too, as well as parents, grandparents, and others who wanted to show support for these young men.

They would be treated to a feast: jerk chicken, salmon burgers, turkey sandwiches, mac and cheese, banana pudding. There would be games of cornhole and paintball and hip hop music.

Most important of all, there was the chance for community, as the young men and their supporters milled about with others in a spirit of togetherness and pride.

One of the proud members of the organization, Deondre Davis, was dressed in a white shirt and dress slacks. He sat near his mother, Sakeenah Davis, who was beaming.

She and Darrell had grown up together in the Union Baptist Temple Church in Atlantic City. She still attended the church. She and her son had been there that very morning. A tech whiz, her son streamed the services for the church.

"As a single mom, I reached out to Darrell," she said. "He's tough love all the way. And I wanted my son to have a role model."

She had reminded her son constantly to be on good behavior and to be wary of trouble, but thought it would be helpful to have another voice of support.

"I told my son that when you leave the house, you're representing your family, your church, your school," she said. "With everything that's happening in the world these days, I worry about him as a young Black man."

Deondre, a high school student in Galloway Township in New Jersey, acknowledged that like many of the other members of the group, he had initially been skeptical about joining Friday Is Tie Day.

But when he gave it a chance and listened to Darrell, that all changed.

"He's like a father," he said. "He stressed that if we treat our parents well, respect others, do well in school, we'll get places. It really motivated me to study hard. And it's paid off."

For a young Black male, Deondre said, it was sometimes a struggle to get past certain stereotypes.

"Other people think we're tough," he said, breaking into a chuckle about his own bespectacled, bookish appearance and slender frame. "I know for a fact I'm not tough. Some people act intimidating because they don't want to *be* intimidated. People act scary a lot of times because *they're* scared."

He planned to go to college and study computer science. In high school, he competed on the robotics team. On the track and field team, he ran the high hurdles and competed in the high jump. He also belonged to a group that mentored freshman students. He even wrote letters to some of the first-year kids, encouraging them to make the most of their high school experience.

"You might not feel motivated about school right now, but it's important for your future," he wrote in one letter. "It's also important for your mental health. You'll meet people. You'll join clubs. We're going to have fun!"

His mother chimed in about the changes she had seen in Deondre since he joined Friday Is Tie Day.

"He's come a long way," she said. "It's just him and me. We've been through some things. But we're still here. And I'm very proud of him."

At the ceremony, the graduating seniors lined up shoulder to shoulder. All of them had been admitted into their school of choice, a list that included Temple, Dayton, Morgan State, Rowan and others. Rowan University was also awarding a $5,000-a-year scholarship to a Friday Is Tie Day student.

With a microphone in hand, Darrell announced that he wanted to say a few things about the name of the organization and the meaning of the tie.

"No matter your attire, you are deserving of love," he told the group. "You should be treated respectfully as Black men. I want to be clear about that."

He said a tie was a signal to the world: *I am someone special.*

"The tie is Superman's cape," he said. "It's a symbol that this is a person who is going to do some amazing things."

Darrell walked up to each of the graduating seniors and handed them a custom-made tie. In turn, each of the students announced their chosen school—sometimes doffing a cap embroidered with the college's name.

They, too, had some things they wanted to say.

"We did it!" one young man called out. "For all of my friends in Friday Is Tie Day—brothers, keep working hard!"

One young man looked squarely at Darrell and expressed his gratitude.

"You kept me out of trouble," he said, and then turned to the crowd to sing the praises of Darrell.

"This guy would take a bullet for me."

When it was Darrell's turn to speak, he was a little choked up.

"I caught some air," he tried to explain.

Nobody was buying it. He was clearly emotional.

"I really appreciate you trusting me with your sons—especially you dads," Darrell said. "Some of you might think, 'I'm here! Why does he need another man?'"

Darrell explained: "I am the second voice—the echo."

He thanked his wife, Janine, and shared one more bit of advice with the Friday Is Tie Day family.

"We've got food, we've got a DJ," he said. "Let's celebrate!"

EPILOGUE

For kids who grew up with financial problems or other hardships, the Give Something Back mentoring and college scholarship program has been a beacon of opportunity. The organization marked its twentieth anniversary in 2023.

Give Back has grown into a national organization, serving students from New York to California. But it began with a single high school, Robert O. Carr's alma mater, Lockport Township High School, south of Chicago.

Since the program's inception, more than 1,700 Give Back scholars—some of them experiencing foster care, parental incarceration, homelessness, all of them low-income—have grasped the Give Back hand-up and excelled in ways they might not have once thought possible.

Some are just now starting high school. Others attend community college, a four-year university or graduate school. The Give Back alums have gone on to successful lives as doctors, lawyers, teachers, business executives and technicians.

"No one in my family had ever gone to college," said Nishena Casey, a woman in her mid-twenties from rural California, born with a cleft palate into a poor family that struggled mightily, and who was a survivor of sexual abuse. "I wanted to be a person who surpassed what was expected of a foster kid."

After joining the Give Back program, Nishena went on to graduate from the University of La Verne. Now married and the mother of two young children, she has secured a job at Loma Linda Hospital as a community health care worker.

"It's been a very uphill battle," she said. "And now I want to help kids like me."

Alberto Davila, who grew up south of Chicago, knew at a young age that his family would not have the money for him to go to college. Give Back and a scholarship changed everything.

"It meant validation," said Alberto, an IT product manager who graduated from the University of Illinois and went on to earn a master's degree at Boston College.

With her father long deceased and her mother in Mexico, Ashley Avila found herself with nowhere to live. A social worker pointed her to Give Back and the organization helped prepare Ashley for admission to college and a dorm room that became her home.

With her credentials, she was promptly scooped up for a position as a medical technician.

"Give Back helps you with things your parents usually help you with—education, therapy, emotional support, just being there."

Dylan Chidick made national news by being accepted to seventeen colleges. He was awarded a Give Back full scholarship and entered his dream school, the College of New Jersey. He became a campus leader, elected president of the student body.

Struggling with chronic homelessness most of her upbringing, Trinity Amankwa earned a Give Back scholarship to the University of Delaware. With her degree, she was weighing graduate school or accepting a job offer as an air traffic controller.

In the Give Back program, she connected with many other young scholars who had faced barriers, and she formed bonds with them. "It shows that I'm not the only one who has faced issues," she said. "It's nice to have that support."

Wendy Puig-Gonzalez used a Give Back scholarship to earn a degree at the University of Delaware, with a degree in psychology and a minor in Spanish.

"My biggest challenge has been to connect out of my comfort zone… Give Something Back has provided me with a network."

As a high school freshman in Plainfield, Illinois, Ronnie Baran lives with his grandmother, who urged him to consider applying to Give Back. He was a bit resistant to the idea, but gave it a try. He said it turned out to be one of the best decisions he's ever made.

"I came from a rough spot," said Ronnie, a diligent student whose favorite subjects are science, foreign languages and coding. "Now I don't have to doubt what I'm going to do with my life. I have a lot planned, including college."

Makenzie Glass was the daughter of a single mother who worked nights in a nursing home. Born in St. Louis, Makenzie grew up in Texas and ultimately landed in the Chicago area. When she was nineteen, her mom died.

In high school, Makenzie registered a 4.1 grade point average and enrolled in seven Advanced Placement classes. With a Give Back scholarship, she attended Illinois State University.

Her goal is to become a U.S. Senator.

Brooklyn Solet learned about Give Back from a social worker when she was in the eighth grade, when she was just coming out of foster care. After a year at a community college, she would transfer to a university with plans to study for a job in the medical field, doing whatever she could to help people.

"To me, Give Back means the word 'hope.' Before, I didn't know how I was going to do it. They've helped with school, jobs, mental health. I feel like I can go to them about anything."

Daysi Silvas was in foster care from age seven until she aged out of the system at twenty-one. Her social worker was an employee at Give Back and urged her to join.

She was awarded a college scholarship and is pursuing a degree that will enable her to teach elementary school students. Her name is on the Dean's List.

"Give Back gives you opportunity... it allows us to be more than a statistic, more than just the consequence of our parents' mistakes."

EPILOGUE

Growing up with grandparents, Gracie Trevino became a Give Back scholar as a high school sophomore. With a scholarship from the program, she went on to Lewis University, with a double-major in theology and history, and plans to attain a Ph.D and become a college professor.

An academic standout, she was invited to present her research paper on twentieth century colonialism in Europe to scholars at Western Illinois University.

"Give Back has given me a wonderful opportunity to grow," she said.

As a six-year-old, Noah Birch watched his forty-five-year-old father die of colon cancer.

As his dad lay in the hospital bed, little Noah would reach up and tenderly swab the man's parched lips with moist sponges. After his father died, young Noah decided he would someday like to become a doctor.

A Lockport High School graduate, Noah would become the first student to go to college with the help of a scholarship from Give Back.

He went on to earn his M.D., as well as a Ph.D. in molecular cellular biology.

Now in his late thirties, he is a physician at Cook County Hospital in Chicago. Dr. Birch also works in research in the quest for a cure for leukemia.

"To see how the foundation has impacted so many lives, including my own, is remarkable."

For kids who could use a break, Robert O. Carr volunteered his time, energy and fortune. As the Give Back scholars and alums attest, it has proved to be a brilliant investment.

INDEX

A

Abelt, Diana, 53
Almost Home, 181–187
Amankwa, Trinity, 199
Ambroz, David, 41–45
American Red Cross, x
Americans with Disabilities Act, 39
AmeriCorps, 39
A Place Called Home, 42
Avila, Ashley, 198

B

Baran, Ronnie, 199
Bartley, Courtney, 14
Bartley, Zebron, 14
Bauer, Alex, 141–143
Bauer, Brett, 141–144
Bauer, Jake, 141–143
Bauer, Lauri, 141–143
Bauer, Scott, 141–145
Beyond, xiii, 44
Big Brothers Big Sisters, 103–106
Birch, Noah, 201

body dysmorphic, 32
Books Before Ball, 9
Bounce Children's Foundation, 19–23
Brick, Sherry, 19–21
Bridgeton, NJ, 9–17
Brigham Young University, 4
Burns, Jack, 107, 109–110
Burns, Joseph Fisher, 107–113
Burns, Leo, 107–113

C

Carlson, Casey, 168
Carpenter, Shawn, 162–163
Carson, Daylen, 190–191
Casey, Nishena, 198
Center for Deaf-Blind Persons, 147–149, 152
Chicago Dental Society, 134–135
Chidick, Dylan, 199
Children of the Fourth World, 136
Chisholm, Shirley, 79
Cleveland, OH, 73–80
Cleveland Plain Dealer, 78
Cook, Pat, 1–8

INDEX

Cool Aspies, 121–123
Cornett, Sarah, 121
Cozad-Bates House, 73–79
Crisis Center, 81–82, 84–86
Czyzewski, Matt, 115–118

D
Daughter from California, 69
Daughter from Texas, 69
Davila, Alberto, 198
Davis, Deondre, 192–193
Davis, Sakeenah, 192–193
Davis, Thomas, 122
Day, William Howard, 78
Des Moines YMCA Supportive Housing Campus, 160–163
Douglass, Frederick, 79
Dreyfus, Susan, x–xi
Duignan, Scott, 187

E
Edmonds, Darrell, 189–195
Edmonds, Janine, 195
Endow, Nancy, 95–101
Engen, Kari, 136
Engen, Paul, 133–137
Evers, Medgar, 79

F
FosterMore, 41–42, 44–45
Frerichs, Darin, 147–148, 152
Frerichs, Kim, 152
Friday Is Tie Day, 189–195
Friends & Co, 1–8
Fugitive Slave Law of 1850, 76–78
Fuqua, John, 9–17
Fuqua, Tasheka, 9

G
Galvan, Adrian, 179–181
Galvan, Sarah O'Malley, 179–187
Gamblers Anonymous, 50–53
Gardner, John, 35–36, 40
Gardner, John David, 36
Give Something Back Foundation, xiii–xiv, 44
Glass, Makenzie, 200
Goldman, Justin "Judd", 127–128
Goldman, Peter, 127–132
Goldman, Sliv, 128, 131
Goldthorp, Judy, 65–71
Gregory, Dick, 79

H
Hammer, Deborah, 122–125
Hansberry, Lorraine, 15
Harris, Evelyn Claracy, 75
Heldt, Brooke, 160–163
Hernandez, Luis, 119
Hope for the Warriors, 89, 94

I
Ifarragu, Alejandro, 121–122
Illinois Alliance for Reentry and Justice, 171
Independence Cup, 129
In Their Path: A Grandmother's 519-Mile Underground Railroad Walk, 77
Invisible: My Journey Through Vision and Hearing Loss, 152

J
Jimenez, Dora, 96–99
Johnson, Magic, 15
Judd Goldman Adaptive Sailing Foundation, 128–132

INDEX

K
Karamu House, 79
Keller, Sandy, 153–155
Kennedy, John F., 57–58
Kim, Young, 129–130
King, Martin Luther, Jr., 79
Kissinger, Meg, 152

L
Lauri S. Bauer Foundation for Sudden Loss, 141–146
Leach, Robert, 78
Ledford, Bill, 81–86
Life Worth Living, 9–17
Line, Kimberly, 35–36
Little Brothers–Friends of the Elderly, 1–8
Lockport Township High School, xiii, 197, 201
LOSS (Loving Outreach to Survivors of Suicide), 111–113

M
MacClary, George, 87–89
MacClary, Joan, 88
Macey, 95–101
Malcolm X, 79
Malvin, John, 77–78
Mandinka, 59
Marquiset, Armand, 2
Marshall, Thurgood, 79
Mayo Clinic, 97, 149
McCollum, Dan, 89–94
McCollum, Daniel, 91, 93–94
McCollum, Jennifer, 89–94
McCombs, Mark, 169–172
Mi Refugio, 136
Mogilner, Cassie, xiv
Munoz, Geraldine, 135
Murthy, Vivek, 3
Mutti, Alex, 25–33
My Sister's Closet, 154–158

N
National Eating Disorders Association, 26–33

O
OAR (Organization for Autism Research), 122
Obama, Barack, 79, 94
O'Rourke, Mary Ann, 107–113

P
Peace Corps, 56–63
Peck Road Water Reclamation Park, 165–168
Phillips, Adrian, 96–99
Phillips, Christopher, 96–99
Pritzker Group, 44
Prospect High School, 115–119
Puig-Gonzalez, Wendy, 199
Purlee, Gary, 37–40
Pursley, Alisa, 103–106

R
Restore Cleveland Hope, 75
Retired & Senior Volunteer Program (RSVP), 36–40
Riedl, Chris, 173–178
Ronayne, Chris, 74
Rowan University, 83, 191, 194

S
Safer Foundation, 171
Sagna, Lamine, 59, 63
Salem Chapel, 77
Salvation Army, x
Schaps, Lisa, 116
Senegal, 57–63
Shultz, Diane, 139–141
Shultz, Hannah, 139–141, 144–146
Shultz, Jeff, 139–141

INDEX

Shultz, Max, 139–141, 144–146
Silvas, Daysi, 200
Silver, Marvin, 149–150
Silver, Ruth, 149–152
Sneed, Rodlescia S., xv
Solet, Brooklyn, 200
Soucie, Donald, 57–58, 61–62
Soucie, Joan, 57–58, 61–62
Soucie, Kevin, 55–63
Southgate, Joan, 73–80
Southgate, Robert, 79
Sperzel, Ceil, 40
Stanford Social Innovation Review, x
Stevenson, Hal, 159–161, 163
Stevenson, Judy, 159
Swanson, Gabriella, 118–119

T

Taylor, Aidan, 21–24
Taylor, Bridgette, 21–24
Taylor, Jim, 21–24
Taylor, Kevin "Bubba", 21–24
Taylor, Kyleigh, 21–24
time affluence, xiv
time efficacy, xiv
Tindall, Brian, 165–168
Trevino, Gracie, 201
Tubman, Harriet, 75, 77, 79

U

Underground Railroad, x, 73–80

W

Wall Street Journal, The, xv
Warner Bros. Discovery, 44
Wheatley, Phillis, 79
Wheeler, Mary, 155–158
William Paterson University, 10
Wilson, August, 3
Wisconsin Council on Problem Gambling, 50, 52–53
WISH (With Impaired Sight-Hearing), 150–151

Y

YMCA, x

Also by Robert Owen Carr with Dirk Johnson

Through the Fires: An American Story of Turbulence, Business Triumph and Giving Back

Working Class to College: The Promise and Peril Facing Blue-Collar America

First Chance: How Kids With Nothing Can Change Everything